JERRY'S VEGAN WOMEN

BEN SHABERMAN

Apprentice House
Loyola University Maryland
Baltimore, Maryland

First Edition

Printed in the United States of America

Paperback ISBN: 978-1-62720-079-0
Ebook ISBN: 978-1-62720-080-6

Design: Sara Killough & Kelley Murphy
Cover Art: Maria Gruzynski
Cover Model: Amanda Jones

Published by Apprentice House

Apprentice House
Loyola University Maryland
4501 N. Charles Street
Baltimore, MD 21210
410.617.5265 • 410.617.2198 (fax)
www.ApprenticeHouse.com
info@ApprenticeHouse.com

For Happy, Chutzpah, and Olive

Contents

Gail 1
Sarah 9
Suzy 23
Missy 35
Mandi 49
Betty 53
Karen 61
Francesca 69
Joanie 83
Josie 105
About the Author 125
Acknowledgements 127

Gail

"Jerome, Jerome, Jerome," Gail pleaded. "You have to challenge him to a rematch. You just lost your queen too early. It was a stupid mistake. Otherwise, you would have beaten him again. I know it!"

"I dunno," Jerry replied, shrugging his shoulders. "Mr. Feldman said I didn't have a chance, if the room was quiet. And it was. You were there. It's not like indoor recess where he's shouting at someone every two minutes to stop horsing around."

"You gotta go for two out of three. Even if you lose, you're eleven! But if you win — that would be so cool. Beating the teacher!"

"Maybe, I dunno. He really smeared me. Like, in five moves."

Gail shook her head, got up from the barstool, and walked over to the jukebox to play her proverbial "Rockin' Robin," "Joy to the World," and "Let It Be." That was her ritual every time she came to Irv's Sandwich Shop. If she happened to have an extra quarter on a given day, she'd play the medley a second time. If someone else's songs had queued up ahead of hers, she'd anxiously watch the jukebox when one of their tunes was ending, trying to will one of hers to play next.

Gail and Jerry had been classmates for the last three years, but it wasn't until the sixth grade that they began to bond. Maybe it was their budding hormones. Maybe it was because they were the only two kids in Mr. Feldman's class who were selected to tutor kids in the lower grades. Or maybe it was because they began to run into each other at Irv's after school and both loved to devour heaping plates of crinkle-cut French fries smothered in salt and ketchup.

For Jerry in particular, the scales began to tip when she started calling him Jerome. Until she came along, he couldn't stand his formal name. Everyone, including his teachers, knew not to call him Jerome, because if they did, he'd lash out. But coming from Gail, it was an expression of affection, and despite his adolescent self-absorption and indifference, he picked up on it.

Their relationship was never consummated physically — they never exchanged even a single kiss nor did they ever talk about going steady — but that might have been why it endured throughout the entire sixth grade.

Gail was a loyal friend to Jerry. She could often be found on the sidelines of his pick-up football games during recess. When he stayed home from school because of one of his many his asthma attacks, she made sure he was brought up to date the next day on whatever lessons he missed. And she witnessed those two agonizing chess games with Mr. Feldman, when Jerry went from feeling like the next Bobby Fischer after his victory in game one to giving up chess entirely after getting creamed in the rematch. Gail didn't cling. She was just present and supportive.

Her parents were both from Italy, which gave her classically Italian features — olive skin, dark auburn hair that ran nearly to her waist, brown eyes, and a welcoming, radiant smile. She was a small girl, and hadn't started filling out the way many girls begin to do at eleven.

Gail had a soft spot for underdogs, especially other students who weren't popular or successful. On Friday mornings, Mr. Feldman led the class in a game he called Academic Challenge in which the students were separated into teams to answer questions about history, sports, current events, music, and other assorted topics. He selected five captains, usually the smartest kids like Gail and Jerry, who in turn picked the members of their teams. As in any pickup game, most captains chose the best players first, and those selected last were embarrassed and demoralized. It was the Darwinian reality of being a kid. But unlike Jerry and the other captains, and to the disbelief of everyone in the class, even Mr. Feldman, Gail always picked the underachievers and misfits first. Kids like Kevin Feifer, who often dressed in fatigues and was obsessed with all things military. He was a poor student and never had much to say about anything; he just sat in the back of the classroom picking his nose and making occasional exploding noises. So, unsurprisingly, Gail's team never won Academic Challenge. For her, the victory was the team itself.

When Gail retuned from the jukebox, the waitress brought out fries and Cokes, and she and Jerry began to munch away and watch life at Irv's proceed the way it usually did on a weekday afternoon. They sat among chain-smoking construction workers, retired Jewish men reading newspapers, and a black mechanic from the garage next door who prefaced everything he said to the waitress with "Hey, baby": "Hey, baby, how bout warmin' up my coffee? Hey baby, I'll take it black with a little sugar, just like you. Hey, baby, ain't I see you on the cover of *Ebony*?"

While groups of other kids came to the diner after school, they congregated in booths in the back. But Jerry and Gail liked hanging out at the bar up where the action was, where they could watch the cook in his dingy white hat and apron grilling burgers and cheese sandwiches, making quips about the Vietnam War and the president. "They don't call him Tricky Dick for nothin'," he'd say to the customers while he worked the grill and deep fryer. "Old Tricky, heh, heh."

Jerry and Gail weren't quite ready to grow up, but they did like their excursions into the adult world where important things seemed to be happening. There had been several fights and race-related bomb threats at the high school in nearby Cleveland Heights, and every nightly TV newscast featured dramatic footage from the war — helicopter rescues with gravely wounded soldiers being taken away on stretchers. At the elementary school, the undercurrent of unrest wasn't being addressed in the classroom. And for the most part, the diverse population of kids — black, white, Jewish, Christian — got along. But outside the school, the adult world was uneasy with itself.

After Jerry polished off his last French fry, he reached down into his pocket and pulled out a dollar bill and three quarters. He turned to Gail and said, "Man, I'm still hungry. How bout splittin' a cheeseburger with me? We can celebrate the end of my chess career."

"Can't do it," she replied. "Didn't I tell you? I don't eat meat anymore. I just can't. No way."

"What the heck are you talking about?" Jerry asked in surprise, thinking that she must have developed some type of allergy.

"Huh. I guess I didn't tell you. Here's the deal. Last Saturday, my Girl Scout troop went to Sunny Acres Farm. We saw the whole place. Pigs, sheep, cows, chickens. We actually got to milk the cows, which was a little creepy…Anyway…"

As if receiving a cue from some omniscient disc jockey, Gail stopped, looked over at the jukebox, and began bopping around on the barstool, as young Michael Jackson crooned "Tweedily deedily dee, tweedily deedily dee" above the chatter of customers and clanking of dishes.

Jerry let her go on for a few seconds, but then let out a big sigh to prompt her to return to her story. Gail obediently continued, "Anyway, we got to pet one of the cows, her name was Josie, and while I wasn't looking, she licked me on the neck. At first, it freaked me out. Her tongue was huge! Everyone laughed. But this big cow was so gentle. Like somebody's dog, but with big eyes and a humungous nose. I just stared at her and she stared back. Then I stuck my hand out to pet her and she licked me again. I dunno. It was just so cool."

Gail stopped to take a sip of her Coke. Jerry looked back at the grill, and then at the waitress, who was writing up a check while talking to one of the old Jewish guys. Jerry was ready for that burger. Maybe he'd ask for two slices of cheese on it.

"Anyway, before we left, Lizzie Davis asked the farmer if the animals on the farm were going to be killed for food. He said yes, eventually, and then she asked him how they were killed, and he said something about slitting their throats and carving them up, and, I dunno. It really freaked me out. I just couldn't believe they could murder that cow. She was so beautiful."

"Murder?" Jerry asked, looking at her increduously.

"Murdered, killed, whatever, Jerry!" Gail snapped back. "They are going to slit that poor animal's throat and then chop her up. Geez, Jerome!"

"Yeah, I guess they gotta do that to make steaks and burgers. But how can you stop eating meat? That's crazy. Do your parents know?"

"Don't get me started on them. My dad is *not* happy, but I just got my report card — straight As, of course — so my mom told him to back off. But she doesn't know what to cook for me. So she's upset about that."

Jerry flagged down the waitress, ordered the cheeseburger and watched with anticipation as the cook flipped it over, back and forth, pressing it down with the spatula to make it sizzle on the grill. Just before the burger was done, he slapped on the slices of American cheese and covered it with a pot lid to make the cheese melt.

When the burger arrived, Jerry dug in. He didn't think twice about eating the juicy concoction in front of Gail. Who doesn't eat meat? He figured she was just going off on another one of her wacky tangents.

And Gail didn't say anything as Jerry ate. In fact, she looked on with a little envy. The burger did look delicious, ketchup spilling over the sides as he bit into it. Gail wondered if she could really pull off this new, radical commitment. No meat for the rest of her life? At that moment, she felt like she had dug a major hole for herself. Maybe she had gone too far. But there were few people on the planet with the will and determination of Gail Antonizzi. While this was a pivotal moment in her young life, she would later take on challenges that would ask much more of her than giving up meat. But for any eleven-year old, this huge dietary change was a big deal.

Within a few weeks, she gave up chicken and pork. For a while, she continued to eat the two-piece platter from Arthur Treacher's Fish and Chips — the only fish she ever liked — but then the local franchise went out of business. So by the time summer rolled around, she was a bona fide vegetarian.

As Jerry and Gail left the diner and turned up Taylor Road, they noticed an unusual figure off in the distance — a kid dressed in what looked like a dark green uniform — walking toward them. They soon realized it was Kevin Feifer. He had gone full tilt; his Army getup that afternoon included a helmet, boots, and a belt loaded with unidentifiable gadgets. Never before had he looked so officially military. While everyone was used to seeing him wearing Army pants, t-shirts, and caps, never before had he looked so much like a real solider ready for action. It was as if he was waiting for a helicopter to pick him up and drop him into enemy territory.

Gail and Jerry were spooked. Was he loaded up with guns and ammo? Everyone wondered if Feifer might snap someday. Maybe today was the day.

When Feifer got about a block away, he stuck his thumb up his nose, fished around inside for a few seconds, pulled out a booger, examined it momentarily, and flung it onto the windshield of a red Plymouth Valiant parked on the street. Mission accomplished.

Gail looked quizzically at Jerry, who was summoning all his willpower not to break into laughter. He looked away from her to maintain his composure. The Booger Incident, as it would be infamously known, completely diffused the tension. But they had had little to worry about anyway. Little did they know, they were actually two of Feifer's favorite classmates. Unlike virtually all the other kids, Gail befriended him. And unlike the many other kids who were unrelentingly cruel, Jerry treated him with indifference. For Feifer, neutrality made you an ally.

For Feifer, this appeared to be just another ordinary day — another day to play soldier. As he approached the pair, he raised his palm up as if swearing on the Bible, forced a smiled, and said, "Howdy folks," with the accent of the guy who runs the general store in Western movies. They both waved back. Gail said, "Hey Kev," and everyone continued on their way.

The next day, Jerry's father, a salesman for three top women's clothing lines, announced that he had gotten a more lucrative territory in Southeast Florida, and that when school ended next month, the family would be moving there. "Better money, better weather," he said. "Hell, Jerry, you can go fishing every day if you want."

For Jerry, there wasn't much anticipation for the move. Obviously, he'd be leaving his friends and the neighborhood, but he hadn't imagined how difficult starting over might be. It really didn't hit him that his life was being turned upside down until the family started packing up boxes, and the long blue and white moving truck pulled up in their driveway. Suddenly, the house was empty, and the family was heading south on the freeway through the rolling hills and farmland of Ohio.

School had ended that year much like it always had with the students getting more and more out of control during the last two weeks. And while the sixth graders would be starting junior high next school year, they weren't thinking that far ahead — not with little league baseball, overnight camp, and afternoons at the community swimming pool in their immediate future.

Jerry never said much to anyone about the impending move. He didn't mention it to Gail until a few days before classes ended. It didn't give either of them much time to think about it. Except for their ventures to Irv's, they were just school buddies, so they hadn't planned to see each other over the summer anyway. There was no dramatic goodbye. During their last conversation, Gail said that Arthur Treacher's had closed, and given that Irv's was nowhere near the junior high, she didn't know where she'd go after school. Jerry realized that that information didn't matter to him anymore. Wherever Gail decided to go, it wouldn't be with him.

Sarah

The first time Jerry saw Sarah, he was futzing with his walkie talkie while standing under the window at the end of the fourth-floor hallway of the freshmen women's dorm. Her room and Rosie's were also at the end of the hall, directly across from each other. He had met Rosie just two weeks earlier at the freshmen orientation party, and she had oriented him well. He lost his virginity to her less than two hours after asking her to share a joint with him in back of the Student Union. As luck would have it, Rosie lived smack dab in the middle of his patrol area. The radio reception wasn't good in her room, so while he was on duty, he had to hang out in the hall where the signal was strong.

Being a student marshal was already the perfect part-time job for a freshman — all he had to do was wear a yellow vest and call in suspicious activity, mainly students who'd passed out from excessive drinking — but patrolling a women's dorm, especially the one where his new girlfriend lived, made it sublime. In his dorm, he was known as Sergeant Sensimilla, because of the irony that he had a campus security job, but with a bushy head of hair and scraggily beard, looked like the consummate stoner. He also quickly gained notoriety on his hall for making a connection to a local pot dealer, a guy he'd met in a small jazz club a few blocks outside of the French Quarter.

When Jerry saw Sarah, she had just come out of her room wearing nothing but a large white t-shirt that fell just above her knees. She was startled and embarrassed to see Jerry just standing there, so she hurried to the bathroom. About halfway down the hall, she turned and glanced back to see him mesmerized by her jiggling breasts and rear end. Sarah was petite, and not as generously proportioned as Rosie, but with no bra and panties on, it didn't matter. There was plenty for Jerry to admire. She looked part Asian, perhaps half Chinese or Japanese, with long, dark brown hair, a small turned-up nose, and tiny feet.

A few seconds after she disappeared into the bathroom, Rosie came out with partially burnt pizza bagels. "Sorry, I keep fucking these up," she said. "I'm still figuring out the toaster oven."

"It's cool," he said. "I am so hungry. I kinda like'm crunchy anyway." But he cringed as he bit into it, the hot cheese having singed the roof of his mouth.

Before they finished the bagels, Sarah came out of the lavatory and scooted back to her room. Jerry tried not to stare, but he couldn't help but catch another glimpse of the scantily clad girl. Rosie acknowledged Sarah with a quick smile. After she shut the door, Jerry asked in a low voice, "Who was that?"

"Oh, that's Sarah," Rosie replied quietly, rolling her eyes, twirling her finger in a circular motion near her head in demonstration of the universal sign for "crazy." "She brought two cats from home. Can you believe that? And in the freshmen handbook, she listed vegan as her hobby. Weird."

Jerry nodded as he ate the bagel. She might be wacky — though he wasn't sure what a vegan was, some kind of witch? — but she looked quite delectable in nothing but a t-shirt.

Jerry's first two weeks at Tulane had been pure hedonism. Daily pot smoking. Daily sex. Daily deliveries of pizza and po boys to his room. And, he was getting paid to hang out in the residence of young women who were away from home for the first time and eager to sow their sexual oats.

His only mistake was committing to Rosie so quickly. He should have played the field. Gone to more parties. Slept around. Experimented, whatever that might have entailed. The first case of AIDS in the U.S. would not be reported for another two years, so the risks of promiscuity were still manageable.

But alas, Jerry was already operating like a married man, spending most of his nights with Rosie, a free spirit from old Jewish money in Connecticut. With far more sexual experience than most freshmen girls, she didn't have the need to lose or prove anything. The fraternity party circuit didn't interest her at all; she had Jerry and his reefer and that was basically all she needed.

Though Rosie did find Sarah a bit strange at first, over time, they became friends, because they lived so close to each other, and Sarah didn't socialize much with other girls on the hall. Being around the dorm so much, Jerry inevitably became part of their little clique.

On the weekends, the three occasionally took the streetcar down to the French Quarter for some beignets and coffee at Café du Monde or uptown to the Camellia Grill for their famously humungous omelets. But usually, they hung at The Boot, a divey bar and grill just off campus. Rosie and Sarah would watch Jerry play pool. He often controlled the table for an hour or two, not only because he could shoot well, but also, unlike most of his competition, he wasn't drunk.

Sarah mystified Jerry and Rosie. She didn't smoke. She didn't drink. She didn't eat meat. She ordered her Boot Burgers without the burger, but with extra tomato and pickles. She was often quiet in public, but sometimes got testy. One time when she was ordering, the bartender thought he misheard her. "You want a burger without the meat?" he asked in disbelief. "I don't eat animals, asshole!" she yelled back. "Gotta problem with that?"

Many men found Sarah attractive — she had an exotic, Protestant-Asian kind of look — but she always got irritated when they flirted with her. It only took a few minutes of conversation with them before she looked disdainful, as if she had eaten a rotten piece of fruit. Jerry and Rosie figured she was just prude.

But she did need someone to confide in, and Rosie was her confidant of choice. A French-Spanish double major, Sarah studied hard and earned excellent grades, but didn't take pressure well, which made Rosie's friendship and support important to her. Rosie complimented Sarah frequently and effusively on her academic performance, though it never seemed to sink in. Rosie concluded that Sarah found comfort in her unhappiness. "I don't think she knows any other way to be," she told Jerry. "She needs to be complaining or depressed about something."

After a few months, Rosie and Jerry had developed their own problems; they barely eked out C averages for the first semester, and their grades went downhill from there. Like many of the freshmen who chose Tulane for its reputation as a party school, they lacked the discipline to do the necessary work to succeed. By March, they both knew that returning to Tulane next year was not in the cards, but their future was uncertain. Would they live together in Cleveland or Connecticut? They both wanted to resurrect their academic careers, but how could they afford to do so? There'd be no support from their parents after their miserable grades. Could they make it financially if they both worked and went to school? Maybe they should both go home to their families, work, save some money, and then reunite in another year. As much as they discussed the options, they had no clear path forward, and the uncertainty of their future put a strain on their relationship. And most significantly for Jerry, the novelty of having sex whenever he wanted was wearing off. He desired someone different — someone black, skinny, chubby, or whatever. He wanted variation. He wanted to explore. But having put on twenty pounds, he didn't have the same confidence in himself he had when he first arrived on campus. And who would want to go out with a guy who was flunking out?

• • • •

Early on Easter Sunday morning, Sarah came to Rosie's room in tears. Francisco, one of her cats, was seriously ill. "He stopped eating and peeing last night," Sarah said to Rosie while wiping her eyes. "Then he began howling this morning. I need to get him to an animal hospital quickly. This kind of thing is serious. I think his urethra is blocked." Sarah was often in a crisis mode, especially when it came to school work, but never had she been this upset.

"I know where a twenty-four seven animal hospital is," Jerry said, sitting up in bed, rubbing his eyes. "It's right by the liquor store the guys on my hall go to. Maybe a fifteen-minute walk from campus. Get the cat and I'll meet you in the lobby and we'll go."

"OK. I'll put him in the carrier and meet you downstairs," Sarah said. "I really appreciate it, Jerry. Really."

After Sarah left, he jumped out of bed, put on his jeans and t-shirt, and began brushing his teeth at the sink. "It's about time I did something productive," he said with a mouthful of toothpaste foam. "I've been with security for the whole damn year, and except for calling in a few plastered frat boys, I haven't done a damn thing."

When Jerry reached the bottom of the stairs and saw Sarah in the lobby holding the carrier, he realized he had forgotten his cigarettes. "Fuck," he muttered to himself, but decided not to go back to get them. There was no time to waste.

Jerry and Sarah stepped out of the dorm just as the sun rose. The campus was desolate, because most of the students were on spring break. The morning was cool and cloudless, unusual weather for New Orleans in early April. Sarah handed him the cat carrier. To Jerry, Francisco's howls sounded horrific, but Sarah said that he always got upset when transported in the carrier, so it might not be as bad as it sounded. But then again she wasn't sure.

Walking as fast as they could toward the pet hospital, they didn't say much to each other — focusing rather on the task at hand. Jerry felt a sense of responsibility and purpose he hadn't felt in a long time, if ever. For the first time, he was trying to save a life. He didn't want this cat dying on his watch. He tried his best to keep the carrier as steady as possible, to keep Francisco comfortable.

During their mile journey, they saw virtually no one as they passed through two neighborhoods — the first of mansions and spacious, finely manicured lawns, and the other of shacks made of loose and peeling wood boards. Whenever he went through these sections of town, he felt like he was in some third-world country. The juxtaposition of wealth and poverty unsettled him. How could these communities exist right next to each other? This wasn't middle-class Cleveland suburbia.

As Jerry had hoped, the animal hospital was empty, so a vet tech, a young, blonde woman in green scrubs, took Francisco right away. Sarah went back with them while Jerry sat in the waiting area. The hospital looked like a typical doctor's office, its walls painted light blue with a few requisite photos of its canine and feline patients. It smelled like it had just been cleaned, which relieved Jerry, because he didn't have his inhaler. All that dog and cat dander could trigger his asthma and end up sending him to the human ER. Wouldn't that be ironic?

Jerry was surprised how concerned and anxious he felt about the cat and Sarah. He wanted Francisco to be ok, not only for the cat's sake, but for Sarah's, as well. She loved her two short-haired black cats; they were like her children. Jerry had only seen them a couple of times through her open door. To him, they looked like two little panthers, prowling the dorm room. And even though Jerry's transportation of Francisco had been the most interaction he'd had with either one of the cats, he was becoming attached to them.

When Sarah first met Jerry and Rosie, she told them how a few years earlier her family had taken in a stray female cat, which turned out to be pregnant, and Francisco and Gino were from that litter. They became Sarah's, and she couldn't stand to be separated from them, even for a few hours in the evening. Jerry suspected that the dorm's resident advisor knew Sarah had cats, which was a major violation of the student housing code, but let it go knowing that Sarah would likely have a conniption without them.

After about fifteen minutes of waiting, Sarah walked out of the examining room by herself. She was sniffling, her eyes red and swollen. She looked overwhelmed. Jerry got up out his chair and walked toward her, but she couldn't make eye contact with him. "The vet said they were going to try a procedure to unblock his urethra and give him antibiotics. He said there were no guarantees, but he was hopeful. He said it was a good thing we got him in here as quickly as we did."

"Well, I guess overall that's good news," Jerry said as he put his hand on her arm. A few seconds later, Sarah broke down. Jerry hugged her as she sobbed on his shoulder. "He'll be ok, he'll be ok," he said, trying to be reassuring. Then he walked over to the check-in desk and pulled a few tissues from a dispenser and handed them to her. As she wiped her eyes, the vet tech came out and told them that the doctor suggested they go home and relax, that he'd call in a few hours with an update. "He's in good hands," the young woman said confidently.

As they walked back to campus, the city came to life. They passed several black families heading to church. The women wore funky, broad-rimmed hats topped with arrangements of feathers and flowers. The children were in suits and dresses of yellow, pink, lavender, and powder blue, which shone brightly in the morning sun. Some of the little girls carried straw baskets filled with bunnies and painted eggs in artificial grass. For Jerry, it was surreal to see people so beautiful and well-dressed living in such impoverished conditions. Back in Cleveland Heights, the faithful were Orthodox Jews who uniformly wore heavy black attire — the men and boys with fedoras and yarmulkes on their heads — when they walked to Friday night and Saturday morning Sabbath services.

"So do you celebrate Easter like that back home?" Jerry asked Sarah, trying to make light conversation to take her mind off of Francisco.

"Not really," Sarah answered with a quick half-smile. "My mom comes from a Buddhist family, and my dad, well, he doesn't practice anything. Well, except golf."

Jerry chuckled. "So are you headed back to San Francisco after the semester ends?"

"Yeah. And I'm not coming back to Tulane next year. In case you couldn't tell, I hate it here. I may just stay near home next year or at least on the West Coast."

"Well, your grades are good, so you should be able to transfer pretty easily."

"I guess."

"In case you didn't know, Rosie and I aren't staying here either. Even if we wanted to, we can't, because our GPAs are so shitty. We'd need to go to summer school full time to have a chance of returning, and, well, that ain't happening."

"Sorry," Sarah said, turning to Jerry.

"Well, we just really fucked up. That's all there is to it."

Jerry was hesitant to talk further about his future with Rosie, namely because he wasn't sure what Rosie had already said to her. He also didn't know what Rosie was really thinking about their future.

Two days later, Jerry and Sarah went back to the animal hospital to pick up Francisco. He was doing well; the swelling in his urethra was gone and he was urinating and eating normally again. And though he was still on antibiotics, they were just a prophylactic measure — the doctor didn't think there had been an infection. He howled as Jerry lugged him in the carrying case back to campus. Sarah kept reassuring Jerry that he was fine. She was touched by his concern, smiling when he commented about it.

When they arrived back at the dorm, Jerry hung out in Sarah's room for a few minutes to see for himself how Francisco was faring. The cat scampered out of the carrier as soon as Sarah opened it, and then stopped and looked around to get its bearings. Gino strolled over, and the cats began sniffing each other, happy to be together again. They were handsome animals — trim, sleek, and jet black, except for a white spot on Gino's left paw. They both had hypnotic, bright-green eyes. Unlike other cats Jerry had come into contact with, Gino and Francisco weren't hyper or skittish. They didn't mind their new guest.

"Hey guys, this is your Uncle Jerry," Sarah said. "Say hello to him. He's your buddy." Jerry kneeled down a couple feet from Gino. The cat walked over and sniffed around him, checking him out. Jerry slowly reached out and scratched Gino on the top of the head. The cat pushed its head into Jerry's hand, purring in approval.

"He likes you. You're good with him," Sarah said as Jerry scratched under the cat's chin.

"Yeah, I like him, too, but I can't do this for long. I have really bad allergies to animals."

"Wow. That's too bad."

"Yeah, it really sucks. Everyone back home has a cat or a dog. But I am honored to meet Francisco and Gino. I know they're you're secret."

"Well, with a few weeks of school left, I think I'm safe. Actually, I think what saved me was Barbara, my RA. Second week of school, I came to her room early on a Sunday morning, because my phone was dead, and when she opened her door, I saw some woman sleeping in her bed. The woman looked older, too — older than a student. So I think she was afraid that if she ratted on me, I'd rat her out for being a lesbian."

"I guess that was pretty lucky for you."

"Yep, it really was. And having you and Rosie as friends was lucky, too. You guys are all I've really had here."

"Same for us, Sarah. Same for us."

• • • •

On the Saturday night after finals week, more than half the students were gone from campus. Rosie's parents had arrived earlier in the day to help her move back to Connecticut, and the three of them were having dinner down in the Quarter. That was one meal Jerry was glad to miss. Talk about a last supper. They were reasonable people and understandably pissed that Rosie had wasted her freshman year at college. And they blamed her relationship with "that pot-smoking degenerate from Cleveland" as the main reason for her academic failure.

Jerry didn't know if he'd get a chance to say goodbye to Rosie. She and her parents were leaving Sunday, and Rosie asked him not to come around during the move. Jerry understood. But given that Rosie might be spending the night at her parents' hotel, he might not see her again — ever. Maybe that would be for the best. Because Jerry and Rosie still hadn't made any plans for their future, their relationship appeared destined to just fizzle out.

Since Jerry was on duty that night until eleven, he decided to station himself outside of Rosie's room for the last hour of his shift — maybe he'd run into her if she came back to campus that night. As much as he knew that he and Rosie were coming to an end, it was still hard to let go. They had been together virtually every day of the last eight months. Jerry wanted some closure — at least to say goodbye.

A couple of girls on the other end of the hall were still moving out at that late hour, but it was unusually quiet. As he stood under the window at the end of the hall, Jerry wondered about all those girls who spent the year in the dorm. Would they be coming back next year or transferring or had they let the hedonistic trappings of campus life in New Orleans get the better of them? The year had gone by so incredibly fast. All Jerry knew was that he had to leave and start anew.

At a quarter to eleven, Jerry got a call on his walkie talkie from one of the campus sergeants. There had been a minor collision between a parked moving van and a passing car right outside the freshmen women's dorm. He wanted Jerry to get to the scene and direct traffic as needed until an officer arrived. "We're a little short-handed right now, so I just want you to make sure everything is under control," the sergeant said. "There are so many knuckleheads out at this hour, including the New Orleans PD. Call us if you need back up."

"Ten-four, I'm close by. I'll be there in a minute or so," Jerry said, peering out of the window to get a view of the accident. As he turned around, still listening to the sergeant on his walkie talkie, Sarah came out of her room, and just like their first-ever encounter at the beginning of the school year, she was wearing nothing but a white t-shirt. She smiled at Jerry and gave a little wave as she walked toward the lavatory. But this time, she moved slowly and deliberately down the hall. And Jerry noticed right away that her t-shirt was enticingly short, barely covering her firm, curvy cheeks. Before Sarah got halfway to the bathroom, she bent over as if to brush or scrape something off of her right foot, completely revealing her ass to Jerry. He could even see a tuft of black hair nestled in the small gap between her smooth, slender thighs. She held the position for a number of seconds to make sure he didn't miss her show. For Jerry, the image of Sarah from behind was sensual perfection. She looked like a goddess. As she continued walking down the hall, she turned around briefly and smiled once more at Jerry. But he never saw her again.

On Monday, Jerry and three other guys from his hall rented a Ryder truck to move home. The good news: Cleveland was the first stop on the journey, because his pals lived in Philadelphia, New York, and Boston. The bad news: Limited room in the cab meant that two guys had to ride in back with the furniture and boxes. Jerry was the only one who didn't go to pick up the truck, so he didn't sign the necessary form to be an authorized driver. That meant he rode with the cargo most of the trip.

Riding in back was hellacious — the space was cramped, stuffy, and dark. Jerry wasn't sure if the truck had bad shocks, or the continuous shaking and jostling were just the consequence of being in a part of the vehicle not designed for human transport. The back door was left ajar six inches so some air could come in, but it also let in exhaust and noise from the tires rolling on the pavement. It was difficult to carry on a conversation, so Jerry and his fellow passengers could only sleep or share a joint and stare at the small sliver of light coming from under the door. The thousand-mile trip from New Orleans to Cleveland began at seven in the morning, and ended just after midnight. Later that night, as Jerry lay in bed trying to sleep, he couldn't rid himself of the feeling that he was still speeding down the freeway in the back of the rumbling truck.

As unpleasant as the ride home was, it gave Jerry time to think about his future. With his mom alone in Cleveland after the divorce a few years earlier — his dad was still in South Florida — she'd be glad to have Jerry back again. Sure, she'd be upset about his grades, but he knew that in a day or two, the disappointment would pass for her. When it came to discipline, she was as soft as parents came. Maybe he'd live at home for six months or a year, until he had enough money to get his own apartment or share one with a roommate. He'd probably need to go to night school at a community college to get his grades back up so that he could return to a four-year program. As for Rosie, he came to the conclusion that he never really loved her. But she probably didn't love him either. They had their good times together — their year of smoking and screwing — but it had come to an end. It had to. They both needed to move on with their lives.

Jerry also thought a lot about Sarah during the trip home. He'd had sex with Rosie more than a hundred times and in every position imaginable — they even fucked standing up on the ninth green of a local golf course late one Saturday night — but none of those encounters compared to the last time he saw Sarah. Sure, she was a piece of neurotic work; it was hard to imagine being in a long-term relationship with her. But that moment she revealed herself to him — that instant of unrequited lust — was so erotic, spontaneous, and improbable, Jerry could never shake the wanting of her from his memory.

And Jerry could never forget the sense of urgency and purpose he felt — the empowerment — as he transported the yowling Francisco to the animal hospital, and the delight of bringing him back home, happy and healthy, to Sarah. It was perhaps his greatest accomplishment at Tulane. And, Sarah's cats had touched him in a way he'd never been touched before. He had found a new connection. He began to see that those humble, loving animals weren't all that different from him. At the end of the day, they were just trying to get along.

Suzy

As Jerry held out the brochure to a woman at the entrance of the fairgrounds, he tried to explain why a vegan diet was better for health, the environment, and the animals. But just twenty minutes into his activism career, he didn't have his pitch down very well. "The dairy cows are given antibiotics, and they're lactating all the time," he said before pausing and opening the brochure to a photo of what he thought would be a downer cow but was a pig in a gestation crate. He kept flipping the panels of the trifold, looking for a cow picture, but realized there wasn't one. "Anyway, sometimes they can't even standup. It's really, really bad."

The woman was a short, stout, blonde wearing a bright-pink halter top that did little to support her enormous chest. She had three little kids in tow. Jerry couldn't believe he was using the word "lactating" in front of her and her children. He tried to maintain eye contact, but her cleavage was like a hypnotic force controlling his gaze.

She took the brochure from Jerry, glancing at him skeptically. "I have some health issues, so maybe I should eat better," she said as she looked over the pamphlet. "You look like you're in good shape. How long you been a vegetarian?

"Honestly?"

"Yes, honestly," she answered, looking quizzically at him.

"Well, it's only been about a day."

"A day? Holy crap!"

"Well, I had been thinking about it for a while, and then when I came here yesterday, and went to the animal barns, and, well it's a long story."

The woman stared at him intently. “And now you’re handing out this propaganda at the county fair?”

“I guess I just wanted to help. The people in this group are really nice.”

The woman and Jerry turned toward the shouting that suddenly came from the other end of the entrance gate. “You get your hands off her motherfucker!” yelled a biker with long unkempt hair, a scruffy beard, and black leather sleeveless vest. He was directing his anger at one of the other vegetarian activists, a scrawny guy in a baseball cap, who Jerry hadn’t met yet. Despite being physically dwarfed by the biker, the guy wasn’t dissuaded and yelled right back. Within a few seconds, the two were on the ground fighting. Four other people with the Vegetarian Action Committee, all women, ran over to try and break up the skirmish. Jerry followed.

The biker was on top of the activist, landing some strong punches to his face, as Jerry and the women tried to hold him back. The activist yelled, “Stop asshole! Stop asshole!” as blood flowed from his nose. The biker also had blood on his face, but it wasn’t clear whose blood it was. Within a minute, three policemen arrived on the scene and broke up the fight.

The biker insisted to the police that the “vegetarian jerk-off” had assaulted his girlfriend, a young woman in a halter top and leather shorts looking on, who angrily concurred, “He was touchin’ my ass and my tits! Guy had his hands all over me! What a pervert!”

The activist, who identified himself as Bill Kyle and a “loyal longtime volunteer” with the Vegetarian Action Committee, rebutted, “I was only trying to extol the virtues of a vegetarian diet to her when Easy Rider over here went ballistic on me.”

Suzy, the Committee outreach director who Jerry had met the previous afternoon, introduced herself to the policemen and explained that there must have been a misunderstanding. “Officers, we’re all about non-violence,” she said. “That’s why we’re here. That’s why we’re vegetarian.”

The biggest of the cops, a young guy in aviator sunglasses with a shaved head, bulging tattooed biceps and a massive chest, listened to Suzy, and looked over the group as the other two officers handcuffed Kyle and the biker. Jerry noticed several families slowing to watch the spectacle as they made their way through the fair entrance gate. For them, the afternoon's entertainment had already started.

"Do you have a vendor's license?" the lead officer asked Suzy.

"No, we're not selling anything, and we're not actually part of the fair."

The policeman frowned. "You're standing here at the main gate handing out this crap to every person who walks in, and you're telling me you're not part of the fair?" he said. "And then your little friend over here starts to inappropriately touch the women?"

"Officer, all I did was put my hand on her shoulder," said Kyle as one of the policemen adjusted handcuffs around his wrists.

"KYLE. SHUT UP," Suzy interjected, trying unsuccessfully to temper her irritation. "Officer, I am really sorry this happened."

The policeman stood shaking his head. A dozen or so people had now stopped to watch the action. Jerry could hear someone off in the distance laughing and singing, "Bad boys, bad boys. Whatcha gonna do when they come for you?" The officer began talking into the radio clipped to his shoulder, saying something about getting three cruisers around to the main gate.

"We're bringing you all in. Vending without a permit. I am not putting up with this shit at a family event. Charge the two guys with assault."

Jerry and the other volunteers looked at each other in disbelief. Suzy, with her hands on her hips, glanced in the direction of the officer, and then turned around to look at the volunteers. She had no idea what to say, afraid that any more remarks in their defense would only make things worse.

Two more policemen walked over, one carrying plastic handcuffs. After frisking and cuffing the volunteers, they escorted them to three cruisers. Suzy and Jerry were put in the back seat of one of the cars.

"This is crazy! I've been doing outreach for six years and never once had anything like this happen," Suzy said to Jerry as they sat in the police car. "What are they going to do, put us in jail?"

Suzy was a cute, svelte woman about Jerry's age, perhaps thirty, with a big colorful tattoo of a peacock running up and down her left arm, and a silver stud just above her right nostril. She had short brown hair with blonde streaks, and wore a tight-fitting green t-shirt with a black and white cow on the front. When Jerry talked to her the day before, he was impressed with how articulate and thoughtful she was. Sure, she looked a bit radical, but she had told Jerry how important it was for the vegetarian movement to reach the general public. "We need volunteers who are respectful and not too preachy," she had said to him when he first inquired about helping the group. "We need to get our message across to people who have been eating animals their entire lives. Too many groups in our movement are busy preaching to the choir, and they don't know how to talk to the average person on the street."

Suzy had been with the Vegetarian Action Committee since graduating from college, and while she went into the grassroots nonprofit with great expectations for changing the world, she had no idea how difficult it would actually be to inspire people to give up their carnivorous ways. Meat-free since the age of fourteen, she believed that once people learned the horrible truth about factory farming, the conversion would be easy. And she was convinced that she was the ideal person to carry the message to the masses. But she quickly found that people couldn't wrap their heads around the concept of life without meat. Despite handing out graphic photos and descriptions of animal suffering — chickens in tiny battery cages, calves hauled away from their mothers to become veal, pigs in gestation crates so small they can't turn around — they weren't enough to alter people's eating habits. Not only did throwing information at people not work, it often turned them away.

Recruiting volunteers was a major part of Suzy's role at the Vegetarian Action Committee, and that, too, was fraught with challenge and disappointment. There were always several no-shows for events and protests, and ironically, the most reliable volunteers were the most radical and ill-suited for communicating with the public. Enter Bill Kyle — a master of what Suzy called "obnoxious antagonism." With limited success, he was trying to become a professional comedian, working with a community improv group, and appearing at occasional open-mike nights. He had his clever moments, but he was more often inappropriate than amusing. Yet, to Suzy's dismay, he showed up at virtually every Committee event, despite her pleas to Marty to have him banned from the group. Maybe this latest debacle would change Marty's mind.

The officer who put Jerry and Suzy in the cruiser walked away without turning on the air conditioning, and the inside of the car was already hot from being parked in the midday sun. They sweat profusely, but were unable to wipe their brows, because of being cuffed behind their backs.

"Marty is going to shit a brick," Suzy said looking through the window at one of the other cruisers. "We've never been arrested. Some stupid shit has happened, but not this. Kyle has always had a mouth. I shouldn't have let him come here. He thinks he's funny, but always ends up pissing people off."

"Well, I don't know if you guys have a lawyer, but my Uncle Mitch can probably help. He does mainly DWIs, but he's gotten people out of jail for all kinds of stuff."

"I guess I should call Marty. He's the executive director of the Committee, but I don't think he knows what to do." Suzy turned to Jerry. "So your uncle is a lawyer?"

"Yeah, like I said, he handles mainly DWI cases, but when I was in high school, my buddy and I were protesting the Three Mile Island meltdown, and we got arrested for mouthing off to the cops. He had us out in less than two hours."

Suzy nodded her head. "Well, that's impressive. He might be a good option."

"Sure," Jerry said, glancing out at the darkening sky. A storm was approaching from the west.

The two sat in the car for several more minutes, incredulous that the police left them in the sweltering heat. Finally, the officer came back, turned on the car and the AC, and told them they'd be heading to the station in a few minutes. Someone had had an apparent heart attack, and that was the cause of the delay. "Once the ambulance is en route, I'll be back and we'll be on our way," he said. "Sorry, folks."

Jerry and Suzy sat quietly watching the line of ominous clouds and occasional flashes of lightening move closer. The fair's pedestrian traffic had reversed direction because of the deteriorating weather; now most people were leaving instead of arriving.

Despite the prospect of going to jail, even if only for a couple of hours, Jerry was intrigued by the novelty and excitement of being in the back of a police cruiser in the company of a cute, edgy vegan organizer. It sure beat his weekday life of wearing a suit and tie, selling modems, multiplexers, and other Com-One computer networking products to other guys in suits and ties. For being his first job out of college, it wasn't bad money, it got him out of ho-hum Cleveland and into the thriving metropolis of Washington, DC, and the corporate life boosted his ego; it felt good to have some disposable income, go to the beach on vacation, and take women on dates to nice restaurants. Last year, when he bought his first brand new car, a sporty five-speed Subaru coupe, one of the salesman in his office said, "This car is going to get you laid, buddy." But after being a sales rep for five years, and not getting much additional sex as a result of the car, Jerry had gotten a little bored with his career.

As the skies opened up over the fairgrounds, the walking pedestrians became running pedestrians, heading quickly to the parking lot for shelter in their cars. Ground strokes of lightning cracked loudly through the air. A call came over the police radio that a couple of power lines had come down near the ferris wheel.

"Glad, we're not out there," Jerry said, "though now it's getting a little chilly. I wish we could turn the AC down."

"Yeah, I am surprised they left us here in the car for so long, but I guess they have their hands full. A storm. A heart attack. And, of course, us — us, the vegan brawlers," Suzy said just before a bolt of lightning ripped behind them. "You know, I was wondering. What inspired you to get involved with us? Normally, getting volunteers is like pulling teeth. To get someone to approach us the way you did yesterday — that never happens."

"Well, it's kind of a long story. You're really not going to believe it."

"After watching Bill Kyle take on a biker, I'll believe just about anything."

"Well, I came here yesterday with my neighbor and her kids, and we spent a lot of time in the barns. The kids really loved the animals. And me, too. So, we're petting this black and grey sheep — maybe a lamb — her name was Wilma, and she's loving the attention. She was like somebody's dog. So affectionate. And she was just shorn, so you could feel her warm skin. Really, a beautiful animal."

"Sounds like you got attached."

"Yeah, I guess we did. So, this guy walks over, I guess the farmer, and we're talking to him about Wilma and how he was showing her, when I asked him what happened to her after the fair. He said they'll ship her off to market and then he went like this." Jerry ran his index finger across his throat.

"Wow."

"Yeah, wow. The kids and I were crushed. So when we left the fair, we came across you guys, and you made a real impression. I don't know if you remember, but you talked to us for a good ten minutes."

"Yep, of course I remember."

"So then when we stopped at Wendy's on the way home, and I just couldn't order a burger. I made the connection that the burger had been an animal. It just suddenly hit me — like an epiphany. Voila, I was a vegetarian. It was as if a switch had been flipped, and I couldn't eat meat anymore. I couldn't believe I ate meat as long as I did."

Suzy loved his story. Why didn't everybody react to the animals the way Jerry had? He got it! She'd been doing activism and outreach at fairs, circuses, and grocery stores for years, but most people didn't respond at all to the group's messaging. When people heard the word "vegetarian," they just kept walking, or worse, they laughed and made fun of the group. She'd heard it all: "kooks, crazies, wing nuts." She often asked herself why she kept doing the work; it seemed futile.

"So what inspired you to come back today and help us?" she asked him.

"Well, I couldn't get that sheep, Wilma, off my mind. I wanted to save her somehow. Short of sheep-napping, this seemed to me to be the best thing to do. You told us that a vegetarian saves a hundred animals a year. So, I thought, 'We need more vegetarians.' So here I am. I mean, it's only been a day, but it feels right. Like, in my gut."

Another bolt of lightning flashed across the sky, but this time, in front of the car and farther away. The worst of the brief storm appeared to have passed, though rain continued to fall heavily.

"Well, I hope this debacle won't dissuade you from doing more with us."

"Not at all, not at all. This is the most excitement I've had in a long time. I'm in data-communications marketing, so I mostly do the corporate thing. So, yes, I'd like to help more."

"Good!"

The officer returned soaking wet. He grabbed a small towel from the passenger seat and wiped his hands and face, then threw it back on the seat. "Well, folks, you're in luck. We're issuing you citations, but we're not bringing you to the station. Too much going on here. Power's out all over the place." He handed them a clipboard with paperwork to sign. "Take the bottom copy. Make sure you don't lose it. It's got your court date on it."

• • • •

As instructed by Uncle Mitch, all the vegetarian defendants showed up to court early and dressed well. Suzy cleaned up nicely; she looked professionally attractive in make-up and a white-linen jacket and skirt, though Jerry missed seeing her distinctive peacock tattoo. In high heels, she came eye-to-eye with him. "I can't thank you enough for having your Uncle Mitch help us pro bono," she said to Jerry as they stood in the hallway outside the courtroom.

"Really, it's no problem," he replied. "He does this stuff in his sleep."

A few minutes before the hearing started, Uncle Mitch, a small, pudgy man with frizzy grey hair and large wire-rimmed glasses, huddled the group together, instructing everyone not to say anything unless directly asked to, and not to say more than what was asked. "Just keep it cool and everything will be just fine. This judge is usually pretty fair. He just likes to keep things moving."

As they made their way into the courtroom, Uncle Mitch pulled Jerry aside. "Look. This should go pretty well. Rumor has it that the judge's granddaughter is vegetarian. Once we're done, make sure everyone gets out into the hall. Help me keep the celebrating to a minimum. The gloating looks bad."

The hearing lasted less than ten minutes. Because the biker never showed, the assault and disturbing the peace charges were dropped immediately. Uncle Mitch apologized to the judge for the group's vending without a license, but noted that the fair's vendor's application did not define what a vendor was, so it was not clear if a license was needed, if no products were being sold or distributed. He handed a copy of the application to the judge as evidence. The officer representing the county, a guy Jerry had never seen before, offered no additional evidence or information when the judge gave him the opportunity. The vending-related charges were subsequently dropped. More than two thousand dollars in fines was reduced to a hundred and fifty in court costs.

Outside the courtroom, Suzy introduced Jerry to Marty who had witnessed the proceedings. Marty shook his hand with a forced smile. "That was impressive," he said, "though I don't understand why he charged us court costs if he dropped all the charges,"

Suzy rolled her eyes. "MARTY, LET IT GO. I'd say we did ok. Just pay what we owe and let's get the hell out of here."

"I'm just saying."

"MARTY!"

"Ok. Ok," Marty said holding up his hands by his shoulders to indicate he wasn't going to push the issue any further. "But listen, Jerry Zuckerman, right?"

"Yes, Zuckerman."

"Listen, we'd like to have you as a guest at the Vegetarian Action Committee for a day. Show you the operation. Take you to lunch. Suzy tells me you're in marketing?"

"Yep."

"Well, maybe you can give us your thoughts on a new brochure we're working on."

"Sure, I guess so."

Marty slapped Jerry on the shoulder. "Great. See you then."

As Marty walked over to the rest of the group, Suzy took Jerry by the arm and led him to the other side of the hallway, away from the others.

"You need to know something," Suzy said in a low voice. "I think Marty wants to interview you for a marketing job. I mean that's what his invitation is all about."

"Really? He hardly knows me."

"That's true, but I did tell him how well you handled the scene at the fair, and with your Uncle Mitch helping us for free...Let's just say Marty loves free. Plus you're a guy. There are no other men on staff."

Jerry folded his arms and thought silently for a moment. "Well, I'm flattered, but I need to think about it."

"Of course. You need to spend some time at the office, if you want to, of course. Then we'll talk." Suzy looked at her watch. "I need to get back to the office and get a fundraising mailing out."

Without hesitating, she gave Jerry a tight embrace, holding him for a few seconds. "I can't thank you enough," she said, smiling. "Call me."

Driving home, Jerry kept thinking about Suzy's hug, how comforting and heartfelt it was. Her appreciation was genuine; she wasn't trying to force her agenda — she didn't have ulterior motives. Wouldn't it be cool to come in everyday to work with people like her? People who were driven by their passions and feelings? Com-One was all about deals and transactions, writing proposals, negotiating contracts, achieving quotas. Ultimately, it was moving paper between him and his customers. He never saw the equipment he sold. He never even saw the people who used it.

And then he thought about Wilma. The poor animal was probably dead by now. Slaughtered. On somebody's dinner table. And that was the plight of billions of animals, which, as the Vegetarian Action Committee pointed out, suffered all the way to the dinner table. Jerry tried to wrap his brain around an image of billions of slaughtered animals, but it was hard to fathom. And he was just one guy. What impact could he really make? And he'd probably be taking a huge pay cut. There's no way a nonprofit could pay him as well as Com-One did.

But with no wife and kids — at least not yet — he could make do with less. And in that sense, he was in a better position than most people to make the move. And perhaps most important, if he didn't advocate for the animals, who would?

Missy

Claire cut the ribbons. Missy tied the ribbons into bows. Jerry attached the bows to the scallop seashells using a glue gun. Missy insisted they make three hundred ornaments — one for each of the two hundred wedding guests plus one hundred extra "just in case."

"Just in case of what?" Jerry asked. "Someone can't make it through the reception without just one? They need a yin shell for their yang shell? An Abbott shell for their Costello shell? An Agnew for their Nixon?"

Claire laughed. "Agnew, what a corrupt prick he was. As bad as Nixon. Do you guys even remember Watergate?"

"Don't encourage him, mom!" Missy said, glaring at her, then at Jerry. "What if some of the shells break? Or what if someone really likes them and wants two or three?"

"I'm sure that any heterosexual male with a pulse will gladly relinquish his sea shell if one of your girlfriends wants an extra one," Jerry said in a facetious tone. "Especially if they'll be used as pasties later in the evening."

Missy slapped her hands on the table. "That is sick. These will be a nice memento of our wedding. People will love them."

"Miss, I think you're shell-shocked. Take a break," Jerry said, as he glued another bow to a shell and placed it in the small pile of finished ornaments.

"Come on, kids. Let's be nice. Just a few weeks and it will all be over," Claire said as Missy got up from the table and stomped off into the kitchen.

Through the entire year-long wedding planning process, Claire had been the peacemaker and the voice of reason. And she found the hotel, the vegan caterer, the band, and most important, she convinced Larry, her ex, to finance the big event. They had had an amicable divorce — both openly admitted their lack of interest in monogamy long before they split up — and out of guilt they did the best they could to make Missy, their only progeny, happy. Though reluctant at first to lay down big bucks for a wedding because of the five-figure monthly alimony he was paying to Claire, Larry gave into her persistent noodging. "She's you're only child," Claire had said. "Just don't get any of your hot little paralegals pregnant — they are legal aren't they? — and you'll be able to afford it."

Though in her early fifties, Claire still turned heads. She was a slender brunette with a long, regal neck, and prominent jaw and cheekbones. She always wore shorts and skirts to show off her smooth, tanned legs. Her skin, even on her face, remained remarkably supple and blemish-free. Besides a few department-store window modeling gigs after she graduated high school, Claire never held a full-time job. She met Larry Hirsch at a party during his last year at Washington College of Law, and like so many guys, he was immediately smitten with her. He joined a DC personal injury firm, they got married, and soon little Melissa arrived on the scene.

Claire became a vegetarian to lose the extra ten pounds she couldn't shed after Missy was born, and became passionately involved in volunteer shelter work for the Humane Society. The Hirsch's Bethesda home soon became a halfway house for lost and abandoned animals, mostly cats, as many as ten at a time. Because of the attention always being given to the animals, and the obvious infidelity of Larry and Claire, Missy often felt insecure and wanting of control and attention.

Claire met Jerry after a presentation he made at an animal-rights conference, and later set him up with Missy. Within a year and a half, they were engaged. Missy, like her mom, was a looker, and Jerry loved the fact that she was vegan, but not all that interested in dogs or cats. Finally, an attractive young vegan woman without the allergic hassle of her pets! For Jerry, it was hitting romantic pay dirt.

But ever since he put a ring on Missy's finger, her issues with control had elevated to a whole new level. And the bickering over the production of the ornaments — a process that Jerry had dubbed "Shell Hell" because it would take several nights to complete — was just one example of the tension that had grown between them. Jerry found it sadly ironic that the engagement, and the decision shortly before it to move in together, had sucked the energy and spontaneity out of their romantic life. Headaches, bad days at work, inclement weather — everyday Missy came up with a new excuse not to have sex. The best days for Jerry were when she was tired and went to sleep early — that at least gave him some time alone to take care of business in the bathroom.

He wondered how they would be faring without Claire around so much; she served as a buffer, diffusing the tension. Claire was thrilled that Missy had found a vegan boyfriend — the first herbivore her daughter ever dated seriously — and did her best not to take sides in any of their squabbles. And the fact that Jerry worked for the Vegetarian Action Committee was just icing on the vegan cake for her. She was constantly bringing over food or taking them out to dinner. It was the best mothering she'd done since Missy was born, and she admitted as such.

One evening during a contentious installment of Shell Hell, when Missy ran out to the store to buy more ribbon, Jerry decided to confide in Claire about his problems with Missy. "We're just not having as much fun as we used to," he said to her. "I thought Missy would get into the wedding planning, but it's a lot of pressure for her. I don't think it has to be. Honestly, Claire, I'm worried that she's having second thoughts about the marriage."

"Jerr, you're a wonderful guy. I can't tell you how lucky Missy is to have you as a partner, and I am to have you as my future son-in-law," Claire said. "Even Larry says he likes you, and he's usually more interested in making nice with Missy's hot little girlfriends."

"Don't get me wrong, you guys are great to me. But it just seems that

Missy isn't happy with me or the situation."

"Look, Jerr, Missy needs a little coddling. She likes to be taken care of. In case you haven't noticed, she's a little high maintenance. I don't know. Maybe do something romantic for her. Flowers. Some lingerie. You guys used to go on fun dates. Take her to Wolftrap for music and a picnic or something."

Claire walked quickly over to the Wolftrap calendar on the refrigerator. "Hey, James Taylor is there on Saturday! Heck, you can take me, too!"

Jerry stood quietly in thought for a moment. Maybe Claire was right. Maybe he should worry less about sex right now and just show Missy a good time. They'd have twelve days of cruising on the Mediterranean after the wedding — there would be plenty of time for some romantic action then. And all the pressure would be off.

"Goodnight moonlight ladies, rock a bye sweet baby James," Claire sang as she swayed back and forth while looking over the calendar. "Wow, Judy Collins will be there next week, too. Send in the clowns!"

Jerry walked into the kitchen to check out the calendar for himself. James Taylor would be ok. Missy liked him, too. But he preferred something a little edgier. Wasn't John Prine playing soon?

"It'll be fine," Claire said, smiling at Jerry with the same big brown eyes as her daughter. As well sculpted as the Hirsch women were, it was the seductive, mischievous glint in their eyes that made them irresistible. How many men had Claire left in her wake? A guy could do a lot worse. And the years had mellowed her, making her even more playful and carefree than Missy. With no husband and her only child grown, she had nothing at stake, except for time spent not having fun.

Claire opened the door of the refrigerator and took out a can of sparkling water, inadvertently spraying Jerry with a light mist after she popped the top on it. He didn't bother to wipe it off his forearm. "Marriage is work, Jerry. I hate to say it, but what you guys are going through is kind of a sign of things to come. Larry and I didn't have the desire or the discipline to make it work. But I think you guys will be ok. You're good kids."

Claire's remark made sense to Jerry, but it didn't assuage his unease. With just a month to go before the big day, his jitters were only getting stronger. At the same time, Jerry knew his fears were as much about him as anything else. He got the same feeling of doom before getting on an airplane or doing a presentation at large conference for the Vegetarian Action Committee. Once the plane left the runway or he stood in front of the crowd and started talking, he was fine, even exhilarated.

Claire looked at her watch. "I need to get going. The cats will be ravenous by now." She walked over to the dining room table, picked up her purse, and then went back into the kitchen where Jerry was still standing.

"Thanks for listening to me, Claire. I feel kind of weird talking to you about it, because your Missy's mom, but there really isn't anyone else I can confide in."

"Not to worry, Jerr. I am glad you feel that comfortable with me." Claire said, lightly resting her fingertips on his shoulder and then kissing him on the cheek. Though she had kissed him before, she pulled away from him more slowly than motherly affection would usually warrant. He took notice of the warmth and firmness of her lips. Jerry felt a sudden burst of energy in his core. Claire gently squeezed his arm, smiled, and then left the apartment without saying anything more.

• • • •

Jerry's first stop at the mall was Victoria's Secret. He'd never been in the store before, and surprisingly, the sales clerks weren't all that hot. He was hoping for supermodels in bustiers, stockings and high heels — a quasi-porn experience — but the employees were mostly average-looking women dressed unprovocatively. One older woman was even wearing a cardigan sweater. That was just wrong to him.

Jerry wandered the store for a minute, too embarrassed to ask for help from the clerks. He knew what he would like to see on Missy, but what would she want? Most of her undergarments were simple — earth-tones and cotton. Would she even go for stockings and a garter? Or would she find it demeaning? Maybe something like a simple see-through teddy would be more her style.

As he rummaged through a table of crotchless panties — wondering why someone would even bother with panties at all if they were crotchless — a cheerful and effeminate male standing behind him asked, "Can I help you? Are you finding what you're looking for?" Just Jerry's luck — he'd been approached by Victor instead of Victoria. Jerry didn't consider himself homophobic — he believed that any person should have the right to marry or screw whomever they wanted — but he wasn't exactly comfortable around gay men, especially flirty gay men at a women's lingerie establishment. It was a real buzz kill. Jerry said no thanks to the clerk without turning around, and then he headed for the exit. Maybe jewelry would be a safer, albeit more expensive, choice.

But on his way out of the store, he noticed a mannequin in the front window adorned in stockings, a garter, pump-up bra, and a g-string — all in black. The dummy's head was titled back, her eyes closed and lips slightly pursed, as if forever frozen in a convulsion of pleasure. Now that was a look. Missy would be so hot in that get-up. Jerry turned around, went back in the store, found Victor, brought him over to the window, and pointed at the mannequin. "I want everything she's wearing. I mean, for my fiancée. She's a size five, about an inch shorter than me."

"Well, certainly," Victor said, grinning knowingly. "Shall I wrap it all up in a gift box?"

"Yep, just make sure you take all the price tags off."

"Well, of course. We don't want the little lady to know everything."

Jerry looked at the clerk curiously. What the hell was that supposed to mean?

As he walked out into the mall proudly toting a pink and white Victoria's Secret bag, Jerry decided to reward himself for his shopping achievement by heading over to the food court and getting one of his favorite vegan splurges — a baked potato swimming in ketchup. A Thai family ran a little sandwich place that served baked potatoes, and they'd always have a long, drawn-out conversation among themselves when Jerry ordered a plain baked potato. They'd laugh, seemingly bemused by the minimalistic request. He repeated his order to make sure they understood what he wanted. "That's correct. No butter. No sour cream. No cheese. Yes, plain, but with ten packets of ketchup. Ten," he'd say showing all of his fingers.

Jerry began to have second thoughts about the gift of sexy undergarments as he sat at a table in the food court and squirted ketchup on his steaming potato. Maybe it would seem to Missy like he just wanted to have sex with her — that the gift was more about what he wanted than her. Actually, there was some truth to that. But their physical attraction to one another was what brought them together in the first place — that and the fact that they were both vegan. So it did make sense to try to resurrect that aspect of their relationship. But just to be safe, he'd better get those James Taylor tickets, too. Maybe he'd wait until the cruise to give her the lingerie. He couldn't believe it — in just four weeks he'd be married to Missy for the rest of his life.

As Jerry dug into the potato and watched the lunchtime crowd milling around the various eateries, he was shocked to see Missy and a familiar-looking woman, perhaps one of her co-workers from the Cancer Coalition office, standing in front of Chiki-Wiki, looking at the overhead menu board. At first, he was concerned that she'd see him with the Victoria's

Secret bag, ruining the surprise of his gift to her. But then he wondered why they were in front of Chiki-Wiki, a regional fast-food chain notorious for cramming birds in tiny battery cages and inhumane slaughtering practices. An undercover investigation had revealed that the franchise's process was so sloppy, Chiki-Wiki's chickens were often alive when they were thrown into boiling water to be cooked. In fact, the Vegetarian Action Committee had organized a protest last year in front of the busiest Chiki-Wiki in Metropolitan DC to demand more humane treatment of the birds.

Jerry was horrified to see Missy and her companion walk up to the register and order. Even if she only got Chiki-Wiki's fries, they weren't likely to be vegan, because they were probably cooked in the same oil as the chicken — a lard-based oil for all he knew. Regardless of what they ordered, Chiki-Wiki was the enemy. How on earth could she patronize those monsters?

Jerry watched a young clerk hand Missy a tray with two containers — the familiar orange boxes that Chiki-Nuggets came in — and two large drinks. A few minutes later, he watched the women sitting at a table, taking the fried pieces of chicken from the boxes, dipping them in containers of sauce, and then putting them into their mouths. The scene was horribly surreal. Missy didn't give a second thought to eating what had once been a breathing, sentient creature. No fucking way.

When Jerry first met Claire at the animal-rights conference, she had proudly declared that Missy had never in her entire life eaten any animal products. Before he set eyes on her, he had put her on a pedestal of vegan purity. And when they made love for the first time a couple of months later, he delighted in smelling, tasting, and exploring her sweet vegan flesh. Though he'd never had a virgin, Jerry was certain that making love to Missy, a woman who'd never had anything animal in her body, was even better.

But a simple three-dollar fast-food order had suddenly changed everything. When Jerry confronted Missy later that evening about seeing her at the food court partaking in Chiki-Nuggets, all she said was, "I don't want to talk about it." It was as if her lawyer had advised her to take the fifth. When he told her about the gift he had bought, she looked at him as if he had lost his mind. She just got angry, told him she was leaving, and started packing a suitcase. In complete disbelief of what was happening, Jerry had no response. When Claire arrived to help make more ornaments, she, like Jerry, was stunned, unable to process Missy's sudden digression.

Fifteen minutes later, Jerry sat at the dining room table alone with piles of shells and ribbons. Claire had left with Missy, and on her way out of the door, turned around and held a phantom phone receiver to her ear, silently mouthing the words, "I'll call you." But for the rest of that Saturday evening — exactly four weeks from his wedding day — Jerry was at a loss for what to think or do. What the hell just happened? Was the wedding off? Was Missy no longer a vegan? Had Missy snapped under the pressure of the looming wedding? Was she ok or did she have a breakdown? Where was she going? More than half the guests were coming in from out of town. Who would call them all to tell them that the wedding was off, if it was in fact off? All those non-refundable plane tickets! What would he tell Suzy who miraculously convinced Marty to run a two-page photo spread of the Zuckerman's all-vegan blowout wedding in the Committee's Action magazine?

Funny thing was, at that very moment, he wasn't sure what he wanted. Marrying Missy, this beautiful vegan woman, had seemed like the right thing to do. It was the next logical step in his life. Who could be better? But marriage, having a family, and settling down had never been a conscious goal — not like it was for many women his age, including Missy. And now she was suddenly unraveling in an unpredictable way. The pressures of the wedding had been one thing — but to start eating chicken without explanation? Maybe he hadn't really known her. Maybe the serendipity of seeing her at Chiki-Wiki had been a blessing. Maybe he should back out of the wedding regardless of what Missy decides. Who would want to commit their lives to someone so unstable?

Two hours later, Claire called. "Missy is ok, I think. I dropped her off at Monica's, one of her co-workers. She's going to stay there a while."

"Ok, but I don't understand what's happening," Jerry said. "We weren't getting along that well, but it's like she snapped. What did she say to you?"

"Not much," Claire said. Jerry heard her sniffling. "Are you ok, Jerry?"

"Yeah, I'm just in a state of shock. Just trying to get a handle on things."

"Of course, I am, too."

"So did you guys talk about the wedding?"

"Yes, Jerry. When I asked Missy about it, she said she wasn't sure what to do." Claire paused, clearing her throat. "Jerry, I don't think it makes sense for you guys to continue, not with the wedding. I mean, it's crazy to go into marriage like this. I know you were going through a rough patch, but I thought that was normal, that you guys would work through it. But this is different."

Claire waited for Jerry to respond, but he said nothing.

"Look, Larry and I can handle all the logistics, calling the guests, the hotel, the caterer. That's really not a problem. You guys need to take care of yourselves."

Jerry began to tear up, but held back his emotions as best he could. Neither of them said anything for the next several seconds.

Then Jerry took in a deep breath and let it out. "Ok, Claire. Ok."

As the week progressed, he came home from work to find more and more of Missy's stuff — mostly clothes, cosmetics, and toiletries — gone from the apartment. But on many of those days, he also found takeout packages from local restaurants in the refrigerator: vegan ravioli, crispy seitan in orange sauce, chana saag, a burrito with a side of nachos and guacamole. The comfort food helped to fill the vacancy in the apartment. He and Claire had exchanged voice mails a couple of times, and in one message, she said, "Let me know if you have any special requests. The eats are the least I can do. Call any time, day or night, even if you just need to talk. I'm here for you, too."

On Monday of the following week, Claire left a message saying that she wanted to stop by on Saturday evening and check in on him. There were a few last things to pick up — pots and pans, the coffee maker, some towels — and maybe they could have dinner together. The thought that Claire Hirsch could be on the make for the newly former fiancé of her only daughter did cross Jerry's mind. Jerry believed that she was capable of such a deed. She'd even flirted with him while the wedding with her daughter was moving full-steam ahead. But Jerry never felt he'd be a participant in such a scandalous sexual pursuit. No way. After all, he was just an average-looking Jewish herbivore, who when exposed to the right allergy triggers, could produce copious amounts of mucous.

And even though Claire arrived at his door on Saturday night wearing a low cut blouse and dark mascara, and smelling like a patchouli factory without proper ventilation, he still couldn't believe that she wanted him. No way. So what if she wore her hair up in a bun, showing off her gorgeous neck? This kind of sexual encounter just didn't happen to guys named Zuckerman — not unless they paid for it.

The meal that Claire brought from Bombay Palace was delicious, though the vegetables jalfrezi was so spicy it made Jerry's eyes water. "I'm not crying over the wedding, it's the food," he explained, getting up to go into the kitchen for more water. "Not that I'm not sad about the wedding." Claire laughed loudly, a little tipsy from her second glass of wine. "You know, we haven't talked about Missy or the wedding the whole evening," he shouted from the kitchen as he filled his water glass from the sink.

Though Jerry couldn't see her, Claire just shrugged her shoulders.

As he walked back into the dining room, he stopped before reaching his chair. Claire grinned broadly for no apparent reason other than she was happy to see him return to the table. He noticed that she had slid down in her seat a little. But also, for the first time that evening, he realized she was wearing dark sheer hosiery. How unusual. Jerry had never before seen

Claire's legs covered, at least during warm weather. He instinctively tracked her left leg from calf to knee to thigh. A little metal clip attached to the top of the black stocking was barely visible underneath the hem of her skirt.

• • • •

In mid-September, Jerry and a few of his friends rented a house for a week at Rehoboth Beach to send off the summer. He loved going to the ocean during the off-season when the crowds were smaller and the sun relented. He had kept himself busy with work since the engagement broke off in late June, and welcomed the respite. The fact that no one brought up Missy during the trip was both a blessing and a curse. On one hand, Jerry didn't want to talk about her for fear of the emotion it would stir up in him. On the other hand, the emotion was still very much there.

On the last afternoon of the vacation, after his friends went to happy hour on the boardwalk, Jerry stayed behind. He went to the trunk of his car to retrieve the box of more than two hundred seashells that had never made it through the ornamentation process. He carried the box about a quarter mile up the shore, away from the small crowd of the day's remaining beachgoers. The surf was pleasantly quiet as it had been most of the week.

He set the box down, and one by one, tossed the shells into the water. He threw the first few as far as he could, but as his arm began to ache a little, he backed off and just lobbed them ten or twenty yards. As he threw the shells, Jerry thought about Missy and Claire, and what a trip he had had with them. He thought about what the wedding might have been like. All those guests dancing and eating, lifting Missy and him up in chairs while the band played the Hora. What would the cruise have been like? Did some lucky couple get to take their place on the ship or did their cabin-to-be leave the port empty? What would he and Missy be doing at this very moment if they were still together? Maybe they'd be out to dinner and a movie with Claire. And then he thought about all those fish in the ocean — billions and billions of them swimming around, eating one another, laying their eggs, doing whatever they could to survive. These shells were persistent relics of their lives, perhaps millions of years old. How amazing it was that despite their brief existences, the evidence that they existed lasted so long.

Jerry began to cry as he reached the remaining few shells at the bottom of the box. By the time he reached the last shell, he was sobbing. He stopped for a minute to catch his breath, noticing how relieved he felt to let go of all the sadness and pain. As he held the last shell in his hand, he thought about keeping it to commemorate the wedding that might have been — the last remaining vestige of it. But no, the shell's rightful home was in the sea, back with all the other shells. And after it left his hand, he followed its arc over a wave and into the water, making barely a splash, never to be seen again.

Jerry stood for a few more minutes gazing out over the ocean. Then he looked at his watch. It was only five thirty. He could still make happy hour.

Mandi

Dear Jerry,

I hope you are back safe and happy on dry land in Washington DC. I hope you don't mind that I looked you up J In case you didn't know you are the only Jerome Zuckerman in the white pages. I hope it is you Jerry! Jerome is a really cool name by the way. It sounds like you were named after a king or a scientist or something. I never met anyone named Jerome before. I think there was also Irving Zuckerman in the phone book. Is that you're dad? So are you Jewish? Do you wear one of those little caps when you're not on vacation? They're kind of cool. I really don't know any Jews. There are like no Jewish people in Winterset. I don't think there are any in even Iowa. My dad would kill me if he knew I was with a Jewish guy but he is such a racist. Are you a lawyer? So whats it like living in Washington? Do you ever see President Clinton or other famous people?

Anyway I know you said that you just broke up with your feance and just wanted to have fun on the cruise but all I can say is wow. You were so awesome. You were so funny when you did karaoke and sang that song Color My World. We thought you were saying Color My Worm and we just couldn't stop laughing. I just about peed in my pants when you told my sister that the good thing about the tofu we had for dinner was that it looked the same after she barfed it up. You were hilareous. By the way I never had tofu before. It was ok. Maybe tofu didn't mix with all those shooters too good. Ha ha!

I hope you don't mind but I am not really vegan. At least not yet. I guess I was for the weekend J See my sister's college roommate is from India and she is vegan and wanted us to go on the vegan cruise with her. You met her. Her name is Saraka or something like that. Anyway I thought it would be fun. I still have to take two summer classes to finish high school but they don't start till July. So I said what the hell. I really didn't get into all those cooking and health classes on the ship. Who wants to do that on vacation. It was like being back in school. But the ship was so cool and going to all those beaches in the Bahamahs was SO AWESOME. I am glad you convinced me to go parasailing even though my bikini top came off when I landed. That was so embarrassing. Being up there in the sky over the blue water I felt like I was in a post card. It made me think I need to get out and do more stuff. Iowa is so boring.

Thanks SO much for letting me stay in your cabin those nights. It was really cool to wake up and look out the little window and see the ocean. It was fun to sleep with you (sex and actual sleep). I know you had trouble getting your little soldier going that first night but I think that's because we had too many shooters J But you were still awesome. I had never been with a guy like you. You made me feel so wonderful. With my last boyfriend it was over in like a minute. He was such a loser. I heard that he was just put in the county detention center for dealing meth. I hate to ask this question. Don't be mad but how old are you? You are so mature but I like that. All the guys I know just want to drive around in their trucks and get high.

So I need to figure out what to do with my life when I finish summer school. I was thinking of moving to Des Moines and moving in with my friend Chrissie. But I am not sure what I would do there. I need to get a job. She works in day care but she also works at a bar on weekends to make extra money. I hope to do better than that. I think day care would drive me nuts. Little kids are such brats! What do you think? I could go to cosmotology school. I think working in a hair salon would be kind of cool. It is sort of creative and you get to make women look more beautiful.

So I would love to visit Washington some day and visit you Jerome J I bet you eat all kinds of good vegan food there. I would love to see the White House and the big statue of Abraham Lincoln sitting in the chair. That would be so cool.

And we could have a lot of fun. I miss you Jerry. You are a really great cute guy and I want to see you again soon.

Love XOXOXO,
Mandi

P.S. Its kind of weird but I noticed these little red bumps in front and they kind of itch and sting. I saw them just after I got back from the Bahamas. Their almost like blisters. So maybe I should go to the doctor and have him look at them. But I hate going to the doctor for female problems. But I have no idea what they are. Maybe they will just go away.

P.S.S. My phone number is 513-555-8791. Call me J I miss you!

Betty

She escorted Jerry through the shelter like a general showing off the barracks for a top battalion. Though she was only four-ten and ninety pounds, Betty Brown projected her voice above the cacophony of barking dogs with no effort.

"We take'm deaf, blind, diabetic, missing eyes, missing legs, whatever," shouted Betty looking at Jerry, who was following behind. "We do our best to keep'em alive and happy. If nothing else, they have a clean kennel and decent chow."

Jerry prayed that they wouldn't spend too much time on the kennel tour, that they would go back to her office where there was probably less animal dander. He kept feeling his right-front pants pocket to make sure he had is inhaler. No wheezing yet, but with all these animals, it was just a matter of time.

Betty stopped at a kennel with a sign that read "Freddy." Its occupant was a small mutt, light-brown, short-haired, wagging its tail and behind so eagerly, it looked like it might knock itself over. When Betty opened the door, the dog rushed out, jumping and barking, its small ears folded back. She picked Freddy up and handed him to Jerry. The transfer happened so quickly, he had had no time to react, to tell Betty he was allergic, that this could be real trouble.

The dog wriggled in Jerry's arms, licking his neck and face. Jerry tried his best to avoid its slobbering, but to no avail. It was the first time in decades that he'd held an animal in his arms. All he could think was: This will be certain death.

"Freddy had a tumor, but we were able to remove it. We think we got it all. He's a real sweetie, isn't he?" She said, looking at the dog fondly, unfazed by Jerry's struggles to contain it. "You should take him home!"

"Sorry, my apartment doesn't take pets. But he is quite lovable," Jerry answered quickly, pleased with himself for coming up with the solid alibi. He wondered if there was a hospital with an ER in this small Virginia town in case he had a serious asthma attack. Could he last a half hour to get a reasonable interview? Marty would kill him if he didn't get it. Betty didn't give many interviews, and Marty had found a photographer willing to do a pro bono shoot. Who knows what kind of photographer El Cheapo found? If the person was free and could find the shutter button, that was good enough for Marty. Whoever it was wouldn't be coming until later in the week. And the way this interview had started off, the photos might be all that Marty would get for the Vegetarian Action Committee magazine.

With the raucous barking coming from all directions and the distraction of having Freddy twisting in his arms, Jerry had no idea what Betty had been saying for the last minute or two. It was obvious he was having trouble containing the dog, so he gladly handed him back over to her. Freddy began barking again and whimpering when she put him back in the cage.

Despite being seventy-seven, Betty looked fierce. Her silver hair was pulled back in a short ponytail, and she maintained a determined squint throughout the tour. In baggy blue jeans and a blue and black, checkered flannel shirt, she looked like she had come straight off the farm. Betty liked being in charge. For her, the shelter wasn't the cause — each and every animal in it was. She made it a point to get to know each resident and come up with a profile for who the ideal adopting family would be.

"Poor little guy. He's a little out of control, but sweet as they come," she said as they walked back down the corridor toward the front of the building. "We need to get him with a family that has kids, but not too small. He needs some discipline."

Jerry felt itchy underneath his chin and on his forearms, where Freddy had licked him, but for now, his lungs were working surprisingly well. Just before they entered her office, he let out a barrage of sneezes, but Betty didn't seem to notice or care. Except for two large wooden bookshelves, the room was sparse. A big window on the back wall let in the abundant afternoon sun. With all that natural light, and a view of a nicely manicured courtyard, there was no need for pictures or chotchkies. A grey calico cat lay curled up in a small wooden chair facing the window. It lazily lifted its head as Jerry and Betty sat down, but soon returned to napping after realizing it was just Betty and another unremarkable human.

"I've been at this nearly forty years. What else do you want to know?" Betty snarled as if an interview was the last thing she wanted to do.

"That's impressive," said Jerry. "There must not have been many no-kill shelters back then. How did you get started?"

Betty leaned forward over her desk, looking at Jerry with concern. "Son, your neck is all red. How in tarnation did you get those big red welts?"

"Oh, I just have bad skin," Jerry replied with an embarrassed smile, checking the voice recorder he had put on her desk to make sure it was capturing the conversation. "Really, this is normal."

"Well, it doesn't look good. That must itch. Can you put some calamine or something on that?'

"Yeah, I have prescription cream for it. Really, I'll be fine."

Betty leaned back, folding her arms. "Ok. So you were asking how I got started." She looked off in the distance for a few seconds, as if distracted by her own thoughts. "My dear friend, Annie, Annie Franklin, lost her husband. He died in a terrible car accident. Came from money, so she was fine, set for life. She had already taken in several stray dogs and cats — they lived on a big piece of land not far from here — and she asked me if I wanted to start a home for these lost and abandoned animals. Sounded better than working for the local insurance salesman. A real pig he was. A perverted womanizer."

While Betty had never come out publicly, it was common speculation that she and Annie had been lovers. Marty had insisted that Jerry ask nothing about Annie, who had succumbed to breast cancer about ten years ago. "Just don't go there. It isn't the point of the story, and she'll probably take your head off if you do," he had said.

Betty continued. "So she bought this building, the Dog House. Paid cash for it. We took just dogs at first, but then she had the smaller building across the way built for cats. We call it the Cat House. That was about five years later. And once people heard that we had started a no-kill shelter, the animals came pouring in. Lots of sick animals that people didn't want to care for. A real shame. It was easier for people to just dump'em than to take care of them."

After a short discussion about how grateful she was to her staff and volunteers, Jerry asked Betty about her vegetarianism. Why and when did she make the decision to give up eating animals? Was there an event or moment that inspired her to make the switch?

"It all comes back to Annie. I don't remember exactly why, but I was invited to a Christmas party that she and her husband threw. I really didn't know her. Practically half the town was there. Somehow, she had convinced Ed not to serve meat. And that's all the people at the party talked about. They thought she was loonie. Sure, there was cheese, and egg nog, and some delicious pies, but no meat, fowl, or pork. Frankly, I thought she was a little eccentric, but who was I to judge? I never fit in well myself. Hell, I was already a spinster. At least that's what the town thought."

She leaned forward, putting her elbows on the desk, folding her hands together and placing them under her chin. She glanced at Jerry for a moment and then looked out the office door as if expecting someone to come in. Her facial expression flattened. She seemed saddened. Jerry couldn't tell if she had finished answering the question or was waiting for him to ask another. She wasn't sure herself, but after a few moments, decided to continue.

"During the party, Annie actually came up to me and started talking about her 'menagerie' as she called it. Oh, how she loved those animals. They were like her children. It's not that I didn't like animals, but her love for them really rubbed off on me. She helped me see them in a whole new way. And she rubbed off on me, too. I never met anyone so compassionate. Still haven't."

Jerry was nodding while Betty talked as if to say, yes, I know you loved her, I know you're a lesbian, it's cool by me. But at the same time, he felt like he reached a line that he shouldn't cross. It would be enough to write that Betty was inspired by Annie Franklin's vegetarianism and compassion for animals at a time when both were considered radical, even though, ironically, the country itself was going through a cultural revolution. Yes, that would be a good angle for that part of the story. But now, he would direct the conversation back to the shelter. There must be some great stories and anecdotes about rescues and adoptions.

Betty however wasn't done reflecting about Annie. She had rarely confided in anyone about the feelings she had for her, and now found herself on a path that was bringing back fond memories.

"Ed was killed later that winter and the shock of it overwhelmed Annie. I began staying with her to help care for the animals and the house. Funny, I became vegetarian without really thinking about it. Living with Annie, it just happened. And boy did I take a liking to those animals. They ate with us. They slept with us. There was one lab named Bolger who took a real liking to me and just wouldn't leave my side. Hell, I'd go to the bathroom and he'd be waiting there outside the door. I guess he had abandonment issues. He could be annoying, but he really grew on me. Yes, old Bolger."

After Betty sat back in the chair, the cat jumped up on the desk, rubbing itself against Betty's arms. To Jerry, the cat's purring sounded like a motorboat cruising off in the distance across a small lake. Betty smiled as she scratched the cat's head.

"So, when we put Bolger down, that really hit me hard. I mean, it was time. He had always had bad hips, but it got to the point where he could barely walk. He was on all kinds of meds, even steroid shots. They'd help a little, but getting around continued to become harder and harder. His death affected me like no other. Not even the deaths of my own mother and father. I guess that's because he loved me like no one else ever had, even my own family. He didn't care if I had a boyfriend, got married, went to church. That's when Annie and I got really close. She consoled me, sometimes late into the night."

Betty looked down, shaking her head. Then Jerry let out a succession of violent sneezes, prompting the cat to jump off the desk and scamper out of the office. Betty stared at him quizzically. He pulled out his handkerchief, wiped his watering eyes and runny nose. "Are you ok, son?" she said. "Be careful with that sneezing or you might knock out a window."

Jerry hoped his allergic episode hadn't ruined the moment. He was pleasantly surprised by her willingness to talk. He had a long list of questions, but letting Betty take the lead appeared to be a good strategy. The conversation seemed destined to move in the direction he wanted, sooner or later. But he knew he was running out of time with his allergies worsening. It was as if a hurricane was approaching. There was a tropical storm warning for now, but conditions were deteriorating quickly. It could be a real mistake not to evacuate soon.

"Sorry about that," he said reassuringly. "Just my allergies. Totally normal. Please continue. So after Bolger died."

"Yeah, after that, I think Annie saw it as a good opportunity to propose the shelter idea to me. How could I not agree? She decided to sell the house and land, buy a bungalow for us to live in closer to town, and she acquired this building, which had been mainly doctor's offices that had moved next to the hospital."

Suddenly, there was a quick knock on the open office door. A young woman in a polo shirt and jeans announced to Betty that a local kindergarten class had arrived to see Petunia's puppies. There were about twelve children waiting out front.

"Little shits," Betty grumbled. "Maybe if they whine enough, they can convince their parents to adopt a couple. Yeah, came in one morning and Petunia was tied to a tree out front. There was a note. Family couldn't afford to keep her. So now we got Petunia, pregnant and all. Who the hell would name their German shepherd 'Petunia'? People. Huh." Betty got up and told Jerry that she had to end the interview, but he was welcome to see the puppies.

On one hand, Jerry was disappointed, because he wanted to hear so much more, but at the same time, he was suffering considerably. It would be a relief to get out of there. Maybe he would call or e-mail Betty later in the week to get a little more information. Hopefully, she wouldn't blow him off.

So Betty, Jerry, and the little shits and their teacher made their way back into a quiet section of the kennel where the sicker animals were kept. When they came to Petunia, she was resting comfortably on her side as her new progeny nursed. To Jerry, the newborn puppies looked like black Guinea pigs. Their eyes appeared to still be closed. It was amazing to him how these tiny, alien-like creatures would grow into large, powerful animals. How great it would have been if the photographer were there to capture the kids and Betty looking at Petunia and her puppies. That alone would have made the story.

The kids, awestruck, quietly watched while Betty talked about how fast the puppies would grow. "In a year, they'll be bigger than you," she said.

One little girl stood apart from the group, looking curiously at the other convalescing dogs. She interrupted Betty and asked loudly, "Why are all these dogs here?"

"Because they don't have homes," Betty answered back even more loudly. "Some families decide they don't want them anymore, and they leave them with us."

"Why would they do that?" the girl replied with a quizzical look.

"I've been asking myself that question for forty years, and I still don't have the answer," Betty said. "It's a cruel world, kid. That's all I can tell you."

Taken aback by Betty's abruptness, the teacher, a young woman barely out of high school, quickly turned to Jerry to see his reaction.

He just smiled back.

Karen

Jerry felt like an amateur psychotherapist. Within ten minutes of meeting Karen Quinlan, he had heard about her sexual-harassment law suit with her former employer; the complications with her father's colostomy; and her beloved mutt, Roger. Jerry tried to keep the conversation on Roger, because the dog appeared to have no gastrointestinal issues or sexual deviancies. Regardless of Jerry's questions — How old is Roger? Where did you get him? Does he know good tricks? — Karen kept replying, "He's a mix, you know. He's a little bit of everything."

Jerry was amused by the fact that this woman sitting next to him at the vegetarian meet-up dinner, Karen Quinlan, had almost the same name as the woman from the well-known 1970s right-to-die case, Karen Ann Quinlan. There was Karen Quinlan the vegetarian and Karen Ann Quinlan the vegetable. He tried to remember what happened to Karen Ann. Did they ever pull the plug? Was there a plug to vegetarian Karen's mouth that could be yanked?

Vegetarian Karen wore thick-framed glasses way too big for her face. Her medium-length brown hair was matted down, and her bangs were unevenly cut as if an untrained relative had commandeered the shears — perhaps her gastrointestinally challenged father.

Despite all of vegetarian Karen's shortcomings, her petite figure was punctuated by large, well-formed breasts, which were made very apparent by her low-cut, button-down blouse. Jerry thought if he got close enough at the correct angle, he'd get a nice peek at her curvy tits. It had been more than two years since he'd been intimate with a woman, so it wasn't taking much to get him going. At the moment, he wanted nothing else from the woman — just a glimpse of her bosoms.

But vegetarian Karen had bad breath, so every time Jerry moved closer to get a better look at her cleavage, she blasted him in the face with a warm, putrid burst of air, which made him quickly back away. And though Jerry was persistent and kept moving toward her, he couldn't hold the position for very long because of her malodorous wind. He was like Muhammad Ali, who during his "rope-a-dope" years, achieved victory by backing away from his opponents' punches at just the right moment. Eventually, the opponent would tire and Ali would go in for the kill.

But Jerry was the one who tired in this sparring of the vegetarians; he decided to go to the bathroom to breakup the conversation. Maybe Karen would engage the socially awkward guy named Willie across from them who did nothing but nod yes, continually bobbing his head up and down. He reminded Jerry of a toy from his childhood — an upright wooden bird, that based on some quirk of physics, would keep bending forward, seemingly in perpetuity, to stick its beak in a glass of water.

As Jerry guided a steady stream of pee into the urinal, he stared blankly into the automatic flushing sensor directly in front of him, lamenting the fact that he was at yet another vegetarian meet-up dinner and the prospects for meeting a reasonably normal and attractive woman were slim. The ratios at these events were always good; women consistently outnumbered men by at least two to one. There had to be another woman, who like him, had strong compassion for animals, but otherwise, had relatively normal habits and interests. Invariably, though, the women were either too young, harbored small colonies of animals which he was allergic to, or were into weird new-age stuff like crystals and chakras. Couldn't there be someone who just wanted to go to a movie and dinner, and have a little romance?

A few months earlier, things had been looking up for Jerry when he met a stunningly attractive vegan nurse named Beth while perusing an online dating site. Jerry considered her out of his league, even before they met. But he gave it a shot — after all, pickings for vegan men were awfully slim — and sent her a message. As luck would have it, she took a liking to him. On their third date, she invited him back to her place after dinner. While they walked back to the car from the restaurant, they held hands, which instantly aroused Jerry — an arousal stronger than he'd felt in several months and which lasted all the way back to her apartment. Finally, I am going to get some action, he had thought to himself.

Inside her apartment, while they sat comfortably on her couch chatting and nibbling on chewy homemade vegan chocolate-chip cookies — she could bake, too! — three enormous long-haired cats strolled into the room. Jerry had never seen cats so big and with so much fur; they looked like feline versions of Sasquatch. He wondered if they were on the same steroid regimen as Barry Bonds. Or were they genetically engineered to torture and kill people like him, the allergically challenged. "You never told me about your cats," he said with a hesitant smile. "Oh, yes, they're Maine Coons. Aren't they beautiful?" she replied. Beautiful like a Nazi death camp, Jerry thought. But he was feeling rather lucky — and rather horny — so he decided to try and stick it out as long as he could. Maybe his allergies would hold off for a couple hours.

But after just twenty minutes of making out with Beth — as the three seemingly mutant creatures looked on ambivalently from various perches in the living room — Jerry began to sneeze. His eyes swelled. Then came the wheezing. At that point, there was no point in hiding the allergic truth. His mucous production and gasps for air were starting to take the fun out of the evening. He had no choice but to evacuate and make a break for the emergency inhaler stashed in the glove box of his car. He quickly found the device, but it was not the same familiar navy-blue inhaler like the one in his medicine cabinet. It was orange, which meant it was circa two or three years ago. Clearly, it hadn't been used for quite a long time. Would it be clogged? Surely, it had aged beyond its expiration date. But he didn't even bother checking exactly how old it was. He just shook it a few times, put the mouthpiece up to his lips and pushed on the canister. But not a hint of therapeutic mist was emitted. He repeated the process twice, but nothing came out. The inhaler was dead. "Fuck!" he shouted to himself in the car. Next stop: the ER.

Jerry figured it would be advantageous to have Beth, a bona fide health-care professional, accompany him to the ER, but all she did was complain about the nurse and assistants. "She should have gotten more of your medical history," Beth whined. But Jerry was thankful they had put him on a nebulizer so quickly; he was beginning to breathe normally again.

Beth continued to bitch about the ER staff and at one point asked the nurse why they hadn't given Jerry a chest x-ray or taken blood. Before the nurse could respond, Jerry pulled off the nebulizer mask and told her to lay off, that it was just asthma and he was doing much better. He thanked the nurse and put the mask back on without saying a word to Beth. He came to the realization that Beth was probably more detrimental to his health than the Maine Coons. It was time to move on once again.

As Jerry returned from his bathroom break, the food was brought out, and Karen and the rest of the guests quieted down as they devoured the vegan feast from the newest neighborhood Thai restaurant. Even Willie the Yes Man had stopped nodding.

The food was wonderfully flavorful and included: spring rolls, lemon-grass soup, Pad Thai, green curry, and some dish that was pronounced something like "gang bang." The motley group of about twenty munched away until after ten o'clock, because there were so many courses to the meal.

After finishing dessert and saying his goodbyes, Jerry headed out into the parking lot to discover that his car was missing. As he walked closer to the spot where he had left his beloved white 1989 Volvo 240GL with 243,000 heroic miles, he saw that it had been parked in a place reserved for a different restaurant in the same shopping center. "Violators Will Be Towed," the sign read. "Fuck," Jerry muttered to himself, stamping a foot on the ground. "Fuck, fuck, fuck."

Karen noticed him looking helplessly at the towing company's sign on the wall. As she walked toward him, Jerry turned to her and groaned, "I can't believe they fucking towed me." She told him not to worry, that she would take care of him. "I won't leave you stranded. Everything will be just fine."

• • • •

Back at Karen's place, Jerry rode her from behind as if she was a broken rocking horse that wouldn't rock. This must be what necrophilia is like, he imagined. She zonked out because he spent the previous half hour pleasuring her with his fingers, rubbing her bulging clitoris, sending her into wild pulsating orgasms. He gave special attention to her prized breasts, caressing and licking them, twisting her nipples hard, but not too hard. No man had ever sexually pleased Karen Quinlan like Jerry had. The few men she had had were real losers — overweight, lumpy, selfish, and most discouragingly, premature ejaculators. So, Jerry was a real treat. He seemed to know what he was doing.

Jerry's M.O. was always to make sure a woman was satiated with pleasure. It was what turned him on more than anything. No matter who he was shtooping, he felt it was his obligation as a man. But more often than not, his partners were sapped of energy by the time he was ready for intercourse; they had nothing left to give him except their nearly lifeless bodies and tuckered-out vaginas.

On this particular late night, Jerry had very little energy left himself. With every hump, the possibility of climaxing seemed more and more remote. And to make matters worse, he was distracted by Roger's whimpering on the other side of the bedroom door. That poor mutt. And he was a mutt. He looked liked a hasty attempt at a quilt with patches of brown, beige, white, and black. He probably had some collie in him, but his face and nose were round, and his tail was long. Not exactly a short-haired dog, he wasn't long-haired like a collie either. And he had been remarkably obedient, not jumping as Karen had commanded, when they entered her apartment. But while the humans were screwing, the dog was lonely and wanted to be part of the fun.

Though Roger's crying and snorting were distracting to Jerry, making it even harder for him to orgasm, he considered the fact that he hadn't had an allergic outbreak to be a major victory. Once every so often, Jerry got lucky and didn't react to somebody's animal. There was no rhyme or reason. When Karen invited him back to her place, he decided to take the risk. He had replaced the outdated inhaler, and as he had once told his pal Abe, finding a pet-free vegan woman was like going to the library and finding the *Catholic's Guide to Sodomy*, third edition. And Jerry knew that Karen wanted him given the way she came to his rescue in the parking lot. After he figured out that the towing lot was closed, she immediately invited him back to her place. "You can meet Roger, we'll have some wine. It'll be great!" she had said. Clearly, this woman wanted some nookie, and Jerry just couldn't pass up the chance to be with a real living breathing woman, even if she wasn't exactly his type.

Jerry continued to go at it as his mind wandered from Willie the Yes Man, to his Volvo on the back of a tow truck, and then to Beth. He fantasized about Beth's tight little ass and big blue eyes. The image gave him a resurgence of excitement. How badly he had wanted her and how badly it had turned out. But at the moment, his imagination was working remarkably well, and he felt a new wave of stimulation move into the head of his cock as he thought about her in her nurse's uniform, pulling her pants and underwear down to her knees, offering him her luscious behind. How tight and moist it would feel inside of her. Maybe, just maybe, the fantasy could carry him to climax.

But then Karen turned around, looked back, and asked, "Are you almost done?"

Jerry stopped, let out a big sigh of exasperation, and said, "I am now. Yep. I am now."

Francesca

At eight years old, Francesca Ward was deemed an art prodigy. The art teacher at her Montessori school called two special meetings with her parents during her third-grade year to discuss the young girl's unusually high level of skill and creativity in drawing, sketching, and painting. Francesca's parents began enrolling her in summer art camps and weekend and evening classes, and always received notes and calls from instructors commenting on her remarkable talent. The young girl was particularly adept at drawing life forms — the human body, animals, insects, birds — and capturing movement and emotion. By ten, she began incorporating abstractions and sometimes surreal elements into her work. Francesca often juxtaposed natural objects in surprising but thoughtful ways. Her watercolor of a tree growing out of a cloud won first place in a statewide children's competition. During the event, the Wards overheard a few parents express their disbelief that a child had created something with such sophistication. "There's no damn way a ten-year-old did that," one mother said as she passed by Francesca's prize-winning painting. "I can't believe the extremes parents will go to just so their kids can win. It's shameful."

While the steady accolades for Francesca's artwork delighted the Wards, comments from teachers about her withdrawn behavior caused them concern. Other kids would complain that Francesca didn't pull her weight during group projects. And while the Montessori method encouraged social activities such as discussion groups and interactive lessons, Francesca usually didn't engage in them. It wasn't so much that she was shy or unable to articulate her ideas or feelings well, rather, she preferred not to. During free time, she sat at a table by herself and drew or doodled rather than going outside where the other kids let out their energy playing kickball or jumping rope. Testing in fourth grade revealed that her math, verbal, and written skills were on par with her peers. But at the same time, the quality of her work was lacking — unless it was an art-related project. The Wards considered psychiatric testing for Francesca, but balked, thinking that she might grow out of her anti-social tendencies. Raising a red flag might just make matters worse. In fact, they suspected that her highly creative nature might make it difficult for her to relate to kids her own age; maybe her lack of interest in social activities with her peers was simply the consequence of being artistically gifted.

As Jerry pulled into a parking space in front of the two-story orange-brick office building that housed the Vegetarian Action Committee and a few other small businesses, he looked forward to a quiet week. Marty was heading off that Monday morning to a weeklong conference in Los Angeles with most other staff, leaving Jerry and Suzy to hold down the fort. Suzy often said that Marty was a better manager the more time zones away he was from the office. Without Marty and his ever-present emergencies and insatiable urges to be involved in every aspect of the Committee's operations, he and Suzy could relax, go for long lunches, and get some meaningful work done.

But a telephone message from Suzy instantly changed the forecast for a stress-free start to the week. "Jerry, I am so sick. I'll spare you the details, but let's just say I can't keep anything down. It's like Armageddon from both ends. I need you to cover my talk at the Montessori class in Rockville this afternoon. My notes are in the Presentations folder on my C drive. It'll be a piece of cake for you. I think they are third, fourth and fifth graders. They'll love you. It starts at one. I'll call the teacher Mrs. Kumar to let her know you're coming instead of me. Sorry to drop this on you. I owe you big time."

After having done dozens of speaking gigs for the Committee, Jerry was comfortable presenting on a variety of topics — from vegetarian diets to animal rights to factory farming — and to a wide range of audiences. But standing up in front of a classroom of kids would be brand new territory, and the prospect of it, especially with so little preparation, made him anxious. Jerry remembered what a terror he and other kids had been at that age. On a few occasions, Mrs. Allen, his fourth-grade teacher, had dragged him by the ear down to the principal's office for pulling stunts like shooting spitballs at the wall clock or making farting noises when other kids were reading aloud. On a field trip to the Cleveland Playhouse, he and his buddies flew paper airplanes onto the stage during a performance. No specific student was pegged with the crime, but the entire class had to draft an apology note, and the school was subsequently banned from the theater for five years. Jerry imagined that if he was a kid these days, a presenter from a vegetarian group would be a prime target for a prank or disruptive behavior. The epitome of cool with her tattoos and piercings, Suzy garnered instant respect from kids. But Jerry looked like any joe off the street, and with no classroom teaching experience and little time to prepare, he'd have a hard time projecting confidence. That would just make him more vulnerable to the shenanigans of young evildoers.

Scanning Suzy's notes, Jerry felt some relief realizing that the presentation was surprisingly brief — perhaps twenty minutes of material — and primarily focused on how animals are intelligent, emotional, and capable of many human-like behaviors. It concluded by noting that people in the United States consumed thirty billion animals a year, and that most lived and died under inhumane conditions. There were no overt messages about vegetarianism or calls to action. Jerry knew that Suzy was reluctant to be didactic for fear that the kids' parents would not appreciate her telling their kids what to eat — or not to eat. The Committee also had a nicely designed kids' booklet with lots of colorful photos and games that he could distribute. If he handed that out beforehand, it might help keep the little devils distracted and under control during his talk.

Jerry arrived at the school promptly at one, shocked to see the two-dozen students seated quietly at four or five tables. They already had the booklets — Suzy must have sent them over ahead of time — along with pencils and pads of paper for taking notes.

The room was nothing like the classrooms Jerry had been in growing up — it was to him like a sanctuary of learning with posters of people from far away lands, easels, paintings that the kids made hanging on the walls, paper mache mobiles strung from the ceiling, a skeleton with a fedora, a periodic table, and three computers.

Without wasting any time, Mrs. Kumar, an older, petite Indian woman with a British accent, introduced Jerry to the class. "We are very lucky to have Mr. Zuckerman here today to tell us about his work in advocating for animals. Just so you know, Mr. Zuckerman, the students will complete a project based on your presentation. They will either write a one-page report or produce a piece of artwork based on what they learn today — it is their choice."

Jerry had never seen a group of kids so well behaved and tuned in. This *was* going to be a piece of cake. Maybe these children had been brainwashed or threatened with a major ass whooping if they misbehaved, but whatever the case, they clearly wouldn't be trouble.

"Mr. Zuckerman, would you prefer that the children wait until after you're done to ask questions, or may they ask them as you go along?"

"Oh, I am happy to answer them as we go," Jerry said. "I like to keep the discussion interactive."

Jerry decided to deviate from his notes a bit and start off with a question. "Does anyone here know what the word 'humane' means?"

After a few seconds, an older Asian girl in front answered, "Doesn't it mean to be nice?" Then a boy in the back in a nasally monotone voice said, "Yeah, like being nice to animals."

Jerry turned to Mrs. Kumar, who raised her eyebrows as if to say, "Look, dude, these kids have their shit together. You're going to have to challenge them more than that. I've already have them solving quadratic equations and quoting Shakespeare."

"Well, I am impressed," Jerry said. "You guys are pretty smart. And you may have already noticed that the word 'humane' is very similar to the word 'human,' and what that really means is that being kind and compassionate are very human things to do. And we should be kind to all living things — other people, animals, and even plants and trees. But my job here today is to talk about being kind to animals."

Jerry paused for a moment noticing that a few children were already writing on their notepads. Then he launched into a discussion of farm animals, and how they care for their young, communicate with one another, and that many are surprisingly intelligent.

"Did you know that pigs can actually use a device sort of like a joystick?" he asked the class. "They push it with their snouts to play a matching game on the computer."

"Yeah, I read that in here," the Asian girl replied, holding up the booklet.

Jerry smiled, shaking his head. "Well, you guys did your homework. I am impressed yet again." He turned to Mrs. Kumar who raised her eyebrows as if to say, "I told you so."

Before he had a chance to return to his discussion of pigs, a girl in the back of the class raised her hand, and without waiting to be acknowledged, asked, "Do people have to eat meat to live?"

Hesitating for a moment, Jerry answered, "No," to the diminutive girl with short black hair, dressed in a dark shirt and pants. She looked almost Bohemian — as Bohemian as a kid in elementary school could look. Mrs. Kumar walked forward a step. She looked startled by Francesca's question.

With some trepidation, Jerry continued, crossing a line he had had no intention of crossing that afternoon. "Actually, I don't eat meat. I don't eat anything that comes from an animal."

One of the youngest boys raised his hand. Jerry nodded, giving him the go ahead to speak. "So what do you eat?" the boy asked.

"Well, I like fruits and vegetables. And, well, I eat a lot of beans and rice and a food called seitan. It tastes like meat, but it's really made of wheat. I also enjoy tofu, which with the right sauce or spices can be made to taste like just about anything."

A couple of the kids giggled.

Jerry glanced over at Mrs. Kumar who was looking back at him intently. "Has anyone here ever eaten Indian food?" he asked. "It's my favorite. It's very flavorful, though it can be spicy, too. Anyway, Indian cooking is often meat-free."

The kids looked at each other, but no one responded to the question.

"Ok, so let's get back to the pigs. Does anyone know why pigs like mud?"

When a couple of hands went up, Jerry felt relieved that he was able to get the discussion back to the animals, away from his diet, though he realized the answer to his mud question was in the booklet, as well.

Jerry finished his talk ten minutes later, and all the kids clapped after he thanked them for being active participants. "And I hope I can see some of your projects. I bet they'll be great," he said. "Maybe I can come back for a visit, or you can send over pictures."

"That's a good idea, Mr. Zuckerman," Mrs. Kumar interjected. "We'll definitely figure out some way for you to see their work."

• • • •

The fact that only four percent of Americans were vegetarian mystified Jerry, the other staff at the Vegetarian Action Committee, and most other animal rights and vegetarian organizations around the country. Why weren't people aware of, and responding to, the overwhelming benefits of going meat-free? A plant-based diet was better for health; it reduced the risk of heart disease, diabetes, and certain cancers. It was better for the environment; animals raised for food were the leading cause of greenhouse gases. And being an herbivore saved a lot of critters; the typical omnivore consumed about a hundred animals a year.

Most frustratingly for the vegetarian community, the plant-eating four percent wasn't increasing much, if at all, from year to year. If anything, American diets were getting worse with skyrocketing rates of obesity and diabetes. Jerry wondered what the hell was wrong with the American public almost every time he handed out pamphlets or made presentations. Why didn't they get it?

Ten-year-old Francesca Ward got it. Just four hours after she heard Jerry's first-ever presentation on farm animals to school children, she refused to eat the bacon on the bacon, lettuce, and tomato sandwiches her mother had made for dinner. "Today we learned that you don't have to eat animals to live, and I don't want to eat animals," Francesca declared to her parents.

Incredulous, Dan Ward looked at his wife, Diane. Then they both looked at their uneaten sandwiches.

"Honey, did Mrs. Kumar tell you that you don't have to eat meat?" Diane asked.

"No, we had a visitor, this guy, who told us about farm animals and how smart they are. We learned stuff like pigs rub their noses to say hello to each other. It's sort of like kissing."

Francesca took the top slice of bread off of her sandwich and removed the four slices of bacon, and placed them on the side of her plate. She put the bread back on and began to eat the sandwich.

"Honey, eating bacon, hot dogs, hamburgers — it's all very natural," Diane explained. "Many animals eat other animals. It's how they live."

"But the animals don't want to be killed. And Mr. Zuckerman told us that they aren't treated nice on the farms. And then they're slaughtered," Francesca explained as she licked some mayonnaise off of her fingers. It would be another few months before she would figure out that eating foods made from milk and eggs also wasn't good for the animals.

"So who is Mr. Zuckerman?" Dan asked.

"I don't know. Some guy. But he doesn't eat meat."

"Some guy who doesn't eat meat, huh." Dan said, wondering what exactly had transpired in his daughter's classroom that day.

Francesca wasn't normally a fast eater, but on that evening, she finished her sandwich and potato salad well before her parents were done with their meals. "Can we have dessert?" she asked hopefully.

"Yeah, I'll cut up some watermelon," her mother answered, relieved that at least Francesca had an appetite and wasn't going anorexic or bulimic. At the moment, Diane didn't know what to make of her daughter's sudden dietary change. It seemed radical for anyone, but especially so for a ten year old. At least Francesca didn't have cancer or muscular dystrophy or something awful like that. But how would she get her protein? She was a growing little girl who had important nutritional needs. Maybe this vegetarian thing was just a phase, and within a few days it would pass.

Dan Ward had argued against sending his kid to a Montessori school, and this was just another reason why. Francesca would have never learned about this crunchy-granola crap at a public school. Furthermore, Montessori wasn't cheap, and it might shelter her too much from the tough realities of the modern world. Sure, there were crack dealers, bullies, and child molesters out there — lots of threats to his daughter's safety and happiness. But at some point in her life, she'd be exposed to the riff raff and need to learn to deal with it on her own. And who was this Zuckerman guy who came to the school? A vegetarian? Probably some Dead Head who was so stoned out of his gourd he couldn't hold down a normal job.

As Diane replaced Francesca's dinner plate with a bowl of sliced watermelon, Dan quickly grabbed the four uneaten slices of bacon and put them on his plate. Both Francesca and her mom glared at him. "What? It's just going in the trash anyway," he said in his defense. "It's perfectly good bacon."

That evening, while sitting in bed, Dan and Diane talked for more than an hour about Francesca's sudden leap to vegetarianism. Ultimately, they decided to wait and see if it lasted. Hopefully, in a day or two, it would be over, and she'd be back to eating what normal kids ate.

"There will always be something to worry about. Before we know it, she'll have her driver's license and she'll start going out with boys," Diane said, sliding a bookmark into a paperback. "It's just never going to be easy. And then she'll go off to college and get married and have kids."

"And then she'll stick us in a nursing home where someone else can change our shitty diapers," Dan quipped as turned off the lamp on the nightstand. "And for every meal, we'll be sucking tofu-flavored Ensure through a straw. I can't wait."

Francesca had fallen asleep right away that night not giving much thought to her new way of eating. Her decision to give up meat didn't come as a result of any lengthy deliberation or the resolution of some inner turmoil. It came quickly and instinctively. She didn't consider how her parents would react nor did she wonder how it would affect her health. Mr. Zuckerman had said that you didn't need to eat animals to live and that was good enough for her. Killing animals was wrong. Causing them to suffer was wrong. They had families. They were smart. They were beautiful. Some could even play video games. That's all there was to it.

• • • •

Jerry thought he had done an acceptable job presenting to the Montessori students, though he felt awkward for not having anticipated that the class would be so well prepared or engaged; they were smart little buggers. He was grateful that they behaved and didn't pull any pranks to embarrass him. He looked forward to telling Suzy about his experience at the school when she recovered from her stomach virus. He greatly valued her perspective and maybe she could offer some advice for improving his kids' talk if and when he did another one.

But before he had a chance to say much of anything to her when she arrived in the office on Thursday morning, Suzy had surprising news for him. "Hey dude, you did a really good job on Monday at the school. Maybe too good," she said after putting her phone receiver down on its stand.

Jerry turned around in his chair and looked at her. "Really? What are you talking about?"

"Do you remember a girl named Francesca? A fourth grader?"

"No. There were about twenty kids, and I didn't get their names."

"Well, I just got a message from Mrs. Kumar. Little Francesca went vegetarian right after your talk. I mean, that night. Her parents are apparently a little pissed."

"You're fucking kidding me."

"Nope. I'm actually jealous that you converted somebody. What the hell did you say to those kids?"

"Nothing special. Believe me. I was just talking about the farm animals — you know, what was in your notes — and they already knew half of what I told them anyways because they had the booklets you sent them. Though at one point, I did come out on being vegetarian. Some little girl had asked me if we need to eat meat or something, and that's when I said I didn't eat animals." Jerry paused for a moment, looking away from Suzy. "I wonder if that girl was Francesca."

"Well, Mrs. Kumar wants you and me to come by the school and talk with the kid's parents. Tomorrow at four. Is that ok with you?"

"Well, yeah," Jerry answered. "But what the hell are we going to say?"

"Just be honest. Tell them what you told the class, and that you didn't even begin to suggest that anyone stop eating meat. And I'll tell them that these unexpected conversions do happen on occasion. Kids will suddenly stop eating meat, because it starts grossing them out or they feel bad for the animals. I can cite a couple of examples where the kids went veg and are doing fine."

"Marty will shit a brick if this family gets really upset at us. I almost feel like telling the kid to go back to eating meat until she's eighteen. Maybe we can take her to McDonald's for a Happy Meal to break the spell."

"Oh, but there's no breaking the Zuckerman spell," Suzy said as she logged onto her computer. "You're the magic man, putting little meat-eating girls under your vegan control."

She turned around, looking back at Jerry. "I still can't believe you did it," she said. "Your first school presentation ever. Jesus."

• • • •

Dan Ward was perturbed that no one could pinpoint a specific comment or piece of information from Jerry's presentation that led his daughter to suddenly become vegetarian. There had to be something that was said — a catalyst. It only made sense. That to him was the first order of business. He wanted to know if there was something that the Vegetarian Action Committee was doing to brainwash these vulnerable and impressionable children. If so, it needed to be stopped.

But before Jerry or Suzy could respond to his questions about the presentation and the goals of the Committee, Mrs. Kumar spoke up. "Mr. Ward, I completely understand where you are coming from. I, too, might suspect that something very forthright or dramatic was said. But let me assure you, that was not the case." Sitting between Dan and Jerry at one of the round tables in her classroom, Mrs. Kumar leaned forward. "Your daughter asked a simple question — and a very thoughtful one at that. She asked if a person had to eat meat. Mr. Zuckerman replied no, and that he didn't eat meat himself. Then a couple of the children asked him about what he ate. He answered them, and the discussion moved back to the animals."

"So what *were* you talking about before Francesca asked the question?" Diane asked Jerry.

"Mainly farm animals," Jerry said. "I think I was talking about pigs at that moment, that they can move a joystick with their snouts."

Diane nodded. "Yeah, Francesca told us about the pigs playing games at dinner that night." Her husband looked at her in disapproval.

"Mr. and Mrs. Ward, I'd like to say two things — one as a teacher and one as a parent. If I may," Mrs. Kumar said. "First, we've discussed many times how Francesca is a quiet student. She usually doesn't have much to say, especially during a lesson. I was surprised that she asked the question simply because she is rarely an active participant in the classroom. So as a teacher, I think it is important to take notice of what she had to say. She expressed herself for a reason."

Mrs. Kumar had everyone's full attention. To Jerry, the fact that she was an Indian with a British accent made her appear more authoritative. She had intimidated Jerry a little during his visit, but he was glad that she was asserting herself now with the Wards. She didn't seem to be taking sides. If anything, she was defending Jerry and Suzy.

Mrs. Kumar continued. "Second, it is not my place to tell anyone, especially my students, what to eat or what not to eat. That is your role as parents. But what I will say is that your daughter can be a vegetarian without risk to her health or well being. In fact, I was a vegetarian from birth until the age of eighteen — my entire family was vegetarian — and it was only when I was exposed to meat during college that I changed my diet. I found out that I loved hamburgers."

Everyone around the table, including Mrs. Kumar, smiled.

"So as a parent, if my child wanted to give up meat, I wouldn't have a problem with it from a health standpoint. In fact, it is probably healthier than a typical child's diet. We have had other students come from vegetarian and even vegan families, and they were perfectly healthy, normal children."

Dan Ward leaned back in his seat, exhaling a big breath of air through his nose. He was clearly irritated, but at a loss for how to respond to Mrs.

Kumar's comments.

"We thought it would be a passing phase," Diane commented, "but she has really dug her heels in."

Suzy reached down beside her chair, pulled out a booklet titled "Nutritional Guide for Vegetarian Children" from her satchel on the floor, and placed it on the table. "If you'd like to take this book, please feel free," Suzy said. "Even if your daughter doesn't go vegetarian, there is helpful information about what a child does and doesn't need to eat."

Diane thanked Suzy for the guide and leafed through it briefly.

Dan glanced at his watch and slowly pushed himself away from the table. "Well, I am not sure what we accomplished here, but we need to get going," he said shaking his head.

As Jerry watched Mrs. Kumar escort the Wards out of the classroom, he felt a little guilty about what had transpired — not so much that their daughter had gone vegetarian, but rather that his talk had helped to spark some turmoil within their family. Never having been a husband or a father, he had a difficult time appreciating what it was like to raise a child and manage their whims and idiosyncrasies. Most kids are inherently rebellious — or at least he was. He certainly had no idea what Francesca was like. For all he knew, the kid was a constant pain in the ass, and her dietary change just made matters worse. And how would he have reacted if some guy from some fringe religious or political group — a Christian or a Republican! — came into his kid's classroom singing the praises of some wacky belief system?

When Mrs. Kumar returned, she told Jerry and Suzy that she didn't have any time to talk, because she was already late for another meeting. But she handed Jerry a watercolor painting of a pig. "Francesca" was written in cursive in the bottom-right corner. "I suggested that she give it to you as a thank you gift for visiting the class. She liked the idea very much."

"Wow" was Jerry's response to the gorgeously rendered image. Though the pig was constructed with realistic lines, the soft splotches of salmon and ivory watercolor paint gave it a soothing quality — subtly impressionistic. Its deep-blue eyes brought it to life, simultaneously projecting contentment and melancholy. Jerry couldn't stop looking at the painting as Suzy drove him back to the office. She concurred that it was an amazing piece of work, especially for a fourth grader. "You really did it there, Zuckerman," Suzy said, "For that little girl, there's clearly no turning back."

Joanie

Normally before going to the airport, Jerry called the airline to make sure his flight was on time. But the last few days had been an emotional roller coaster, to say the least, so it never crossed his mind. And if there happened to be a flight delay or a cancellation it was, of course, a headache. But there Jerry stood at the United Airlines ticket counter at the Portland airport with a big grin after the agent told him that his flight was cancelled, and she'd have to book him on the same flight out tomorrow. Jerry was thrilled, because he could now return to the hotel and re-unite with Joanie.

So he called Pete's Taxi Service for the ride back to the Embassy Suites. The hotel had a deal with Pete who prided himself on his small fleet of clean, comfortable cars and customer-oriented drivers. It happened to be Pete who brought Jerry to the hotel from the airport when he flew in three days ago, and now it was Pete who was picking him up to take him back downtown.

With Pete, you got more than just a ride from point A to point B. He could be your tour guide, city historian, or local political analyst. He even knew where "a guy could get a nice rub down with a happy ending," because, "Every guy deserves a happy ending. Life's too short."

When Pete picked up someone successful — a businessperson, doctor, or lawyer — he'd often launch into his own life story as a way of saying, "Yeah, I've been there, I've had a piece of the pie, traveling and making money just like you. I'm *somebody*." And when he first picked up Jerry and learned he was making a presentation on the environment at the Vegetarian Action Conference, the conversation strayed into Pete's stint in Vietnam loading bombs into B-52s and some sort of military consulting after his honorable discharge. After that career, and a couple of ex-wives, he began his most rewarding work — psychotherapy.

"Hard to tell if I was really helping people, you know, saving their marriages, but they seemed to get something from the sessions. You know, a catharsis or a revelation. I came to the conclusion that it's hard to get someone to change. But if I could help them understand who they were and why they were the way they were, that meant something. It was progress."

As Pete yammered on about his take on the human condition, Jerry wondered how the fuck this guy ended up as a therapist. Did Pete even go to college? How many ex-wives did he have? But then again, Freud was a sex-obsessed cocaine addict. If Freud could do it, why not this cab driver? And what Pete said did make sense. Happiness and harmony among friends, lovers, whomever is often elusive. As Pete concluded, "Sometimes you just have to do the best you can do and then call it a day. If the relationship doesn't work out, at least you gave it a decent shot."

Jerry was happy to see Pete again — a friendly and familiar face. So much had happened in the past three days. Maybe he could talk to Pete about the strange circumstances with Joanie.

"Hey buddy. You just couldn't leave Portland, eh?" said Pete as Jerry plopped down on the roomy backseat of the cab. "Problem with your flight?"

"Yeah, they cancelled it. Not sure why. Obviously the weather's fine here. But I guess that doesn't really matter. The bottom line is: I'm not going anywhere except back downtown."

"Well, it is a beautiful fall day, so maybe you can find something to do down by the river. You know, enjoy yourself."

Little had the cabbie known what an incredible time he had already had. Jerry decided to tell him about it. Maybe Pete could provide perspective — an unemotional, objective, and maybe even informed opinion. What did he have to lose?

Jerry couldn't help but think something metaphysical or mystical might have been happening. How poetic, how fortuitous for his flight to be cancelled giving him the chance to finish something that had seemed to be left completely unresolved. Jerry and Joanie had made no plans or arrangements for moving forward after their three days together. No one promised to call or write. Would they ever talk again? But now fate, dumb luck, or whatever you want to call it, was bringing him back to her.

So in a half hour, he'd come back to her room, knock on her door, and then what?

• • • •

Three days earlier, Jerry stood in front of about thirty conference attendees confidently breezing through his PowerPoint slides with facts and information on how a vegetarian or vegan diet — or just cutting back on animal products — could substantially reduce greenhouse gases, and, of course, save a lot of animals.

"Let's do a little math. There are about three hundred million people in the U.S. Each consumes about one hundred animals a year. So that's a total of thirty billion animals. Imagine if everyone cut back by ten or twenty percent. We'd save tens of millions of animals and make a meaningful reduction in which harmful gas?"

He had asked that question three times during his presentation, in part to be a little humorous, but also so the attendees would remember the name of the culprit gas and go back to their local groups and communities and speak knowledgably about the issue.

Some guy from the back row shouted sarcastically, "If I am not mistaken, Jerr, I believe that would be methane."

"We have a winner," Jerry replied. "Yes, methane."

On the left-hand side of Jerry's next slide was an image of cows huddled together in a pen. The animals look agitated, even spooked. Jerry didn't know for certain, but the photo might have been taken just before a slaughter. On the right-hand side of the slide was a photo of the earth shrouded in haze. "Methane Madness" was the caption at the top. "Silent But Deadly" ran across the bottom.

"This is my last slide of the session. Kudos to my colleague Carla from Veg Action who created this poster. I brought a few with me as parting gifts for you, but you can also order them online. They're free. You just pay for shipping. Also, we have Methane Madness whoopee cushions, which as you can imagine are really popular with the kids. They can cause a real stink. I mean, really. You've been forewarned. Anyway, thanks for taking time to listen to me. I do appreciate it."

They weren't exactly fans at Camden Yards after a Cal Ripken walk-off home run, but Jerry was pleased with the enthusiastic applause he got from the small group. A couple of people made a bee line to the table with the posters and whoopee cushions, and within a minute, the give-aways were all gone.

A haggard woman carrying four stuffed bags approached Jerry as he was logging out of his laptop. She wore baggy royal-blue sweatpants and a washed-out maroon t-shirt. Must be a hoarder, Jerry thought. Probably no fewer than a dozen cats in her house.

"Excuse me. I have a question. I read on the Internet that you should wash all vegetables in bleach," she said. "Have you heard of this? Gets rid of the pesticides and toxins. Do you know how much bleach I should use?"

"You know, I'm not an expert in food preparation. Sounds kind of extreme to me."

Jerry noticed that waiting behind the hoarder was an earthy-looking woman with long and bushy black hair. She wore a bright pink and yellow madras shirt and faded jeans. She smiled knowingly at Jerry, acknowledging his awkward moment with the eccentric woman.

"Do you know where I can get more information on bleaching vegetables?" the hoarder asked again.

"Look, ma'am, bleach is nasty stuff. It's poison. I honestly don't think it makes much sense."

The hoarder paused and looked at Jerry in frustration. "Ok, then. Where can I get one of those methane posters?"

"Here, you can have mine," interjected the woman behind her. "I'm gonna order a bunch online anyway. Really, it's ok."

The hoarder said thank you, took the poster, and searched for a place in one of her bags to stuff it. As she bent over, nearly her entire ass popped out of the loose sweat pants. It seemed to hover in plain view for several seconds. She nonchalantly pulled her sweat pants back up, gathered her bags, and walked away.

"Well that was different," said Joanie, chuckling and pulling her hair away from her face. She turned pink from the embarrassment of having seen the hoarder's behind.

"Just say no to crack," quipped Jerry.

"And bleaching your vegetables!"

"Yeah, I think you're right on that. I am amazed by the stuff people come up with."

She nodded and smiled broadly. "I know, I know! Anyway, I'm Joanie Sanders. I teach a group of special kids in upstate New York, and they would love your poster. I'll have to think about the whoopee cushions. They can get so out of control with stuff like that. Don't get me wrong. They're great kids and they get the vegetarian thing. They're not vegetarian themselves, at least not yet, but they really care about the animals."

"We love it when kids get excited about the animals," Jerry replied. "After all, the kids are the future."

Joanie nodded, though her smile flattened slightly, as if she'd become saddened by the comment.

Jerry handed her his card, showing her the URL for ordering the posters, and then thanked her for coming. During the exchange, he noticed her well-endowed engagement ring, at least two carats, maybe three.

"Hey, thank you. How can you beat a presentation with whoopee cushions?" Joanie said before picking up her backpack and leaving the room.

As Jerry shut down his laptop, he envisioned Joanie at work with the special-needs kids — helping them with their projects, being patient and supportive, teaching them to be compassionate, and building their self esteem and independence. Her smile was genuine and disarming. The kids must really warm up to her.

Joanie did in fact have a gift for immediately and unequivocally building trust with everyone around her — kids or adults. She frequently touched people lightly on the forearm when delivering a compliment or expressing appreciation. It was as if she cast an unbreakable spell that forever connected the recipient to her. Rarely did anyone doubt her intentions, and rarely was she selfish. Before becoming a teacher, Joanie worked as a school nurse, and virtually every child that came into her clinic walked away with the joy that comes with making a new friend.

But Jerry's attention quickly turned to attending the next presentation, an expert panel on factory farming and the environment. Marty wanted him to be there. In fact, it was the only presentation he'd asked Jerry to see. "If there's any new legislation or data, it will come out of that group, so make sure you're there," Marty had said. So Jerry packed up his equipment as quickly as he could. After that session, he'd have no other commitments the rest of the weekend. Maybe he could sneak away later and have some fun.

• • • •

When Joanie got in the long line for the conference's buffet vegan lunch, the woman in front of her warned her that the hotel was already running out food. The woman had heard that they had miscalculated the headcount and were scrambling to get more of the tofu burrito entrees out as quickly as possible. "But we've been here for ten minutes and the line hasn't moved," the woman said. "This really sucks. Then when the food does come, we'll have no time to eat it."

Joanie left, and after seeing a waiting line for the hotel restaurant, she headed for the bar, and took a table off in a corner. She didn't even bother looking at a menu. She went up to the bartender and ordered fries and a Coke, asking him to make sure the fries were cooked in vegetable oil. Except for the voice of the CNN anchorwoman on the TV above the bar, the place was quiet and empty, and for Joanie, unusually relaxing. No kids. No parents. None of her husband's friends over to watch the Yankees on TV. It was strange, even surreal, for her to be alone in the middle of the day, especially in a hotel bar on the other side of the country. Joanie and Dan rarely travelled. Between her teaching schedule and his thriving computer-security consulting business, they never had time for vacation. Once in a while they'd go into Manhattan to meet friends for dinner and a show, but rarely ventured anywhere farther away. Before this trip, Joanie realized she hadn't even been on an airplane for five or six years.

While waiting for her order to arrive, she leafed through the conference program. On almost every page was a photo of a suffering animal. A downer dairy cow unable to stand. A caged calf destined to become veal. A pit bull, its face bloodied and mangled from fighting. A trainer with a whip standing in front of shackled circus elephant. On one hand, she was glad to be at the conference to learn more about the myriad issues that animals face and present it later to the new vegetarian group at her Unitarian church. On the other hand, it was depressing. All these rescue groups, humane societies, shelters, and sanctuaries worked tirelessly for what were usually only incremental victories. Even her kids, who struggled to fit into mainstream society because of developmental disabilities like autism and Down syndrome, had it pretty damn good compared to the animals.

As Jerry headed back to his room to check his e-mail, he passed by the bar and noticed Joanie sitting alone, the only patron. On impulse, he decided to go in and say hello. He had no other conscious intention at that moment. And Joanie was glad to see him, a friendly face, a diversion from the pictures of plighted animals. Her order arrived just as Jerry did, so she asked him to sit down and share the oversized plate of steak fries.

"Please join me. This is humungous. I'll never finish them myself," she said. "If you don't, I'll have to donate them to the conference. I don't know if you heard, but they ran out of food. People are *pissed.*"

Jerry laughed as he sat down. Joanie pushed the plate of fries between them, politely insisting that he partake.

"You know, I thought about it, and I'm gonna get some of those whoopee cushions after all. I'll bribe the kids with them. Use them as prizes. Rewards for extra credit. That kinda stuff. Their parents might kill me for it, but well, whatever. They'll get over it."

Jerry ordered a Coke, and the two of them methodically ate the monster fries while they discussed the meetings and presentations. Joanie admitted to being a little depressed by the conference and the subject matter. "There just isn't a whole lot of feel-good material in here," she said, holding up the program. "Don't get me wrong. People are doing incredible things to help the animals, but honestly, it's hard tell how much of a difference they're making."

Jerry agreed. "You're right. I guess I hope for a day when the public will suddenly 'get it' and everyone will go vegetarian. I know that's wishful thinking. But until then, we just need to keep getting the word out."

The more they talked, the more Jerry appreciated Joanie for being unlike most of the conference attendees, and for that matter, most vegetarians. She wasn't too serious or idealistic, and she didn't have a pretentious or self-righteous bone in her body. She had no facade. She even laughed a lot.

When Jerry asked a woman to do something or go on a date, he had to summon some courage. But he felt so comfortable with her. Without any second thought, he asked her to play hooky from the conference with him that afternoon and go venturing outside. "You know what we should do?" he said. "We should blow this pop stand and enjoy the outdoors. It's such a beautiful day. There's some type of festival down by the river. I'm not sure what it is. But there are tents and music."

"Wow," Joanie said, "That sounds *so good*." Then she paused and looked down at the empty plate. "I really shouldn't. My Unitarian church group helped pay for me to come here. I'm supposed to report back to them."

"Really? Well, it'll only be for the afternoon. You'll have all day Saturday and most of Sunday to get information." Then he hesitated. "But don't let me push you. I completely understand if you can't. And, I know those Unitarians can be a wicked lot. You don't want to piss them off."

"They're just a bunch of old hippies. But I guess that's what I am."

"Quite the contrary. You're just a middle-aged hippie."

"Bastard," Joanie said, feigning anger. "I bet you're older than me."

"Let's not go there. Let's just say I'm a middle-aged hippie, too."

Leaving the conference and going outdoors was so tempting for Joanie. But who was this Jerry guy? He seemed smart and funny, even kind of cute. But she didn't want to lead him on. She noticed earlier that he didn't have a wedding band. She decided to level with him, and see how he responded. Maybe she'd go.

"Look. It sounds like a great time. But I just want you to know I'm married. Happily." Then she looked over toward the bright sunshine coming down the hall through the front door of the hotel.

Jerry leaned back in his chair. "No problem. Honestly, I do these conferences all the time. I'm a little burnt out on them. I just want to breathe a little fresh air. And Portland is so beautiful. Why not enjoy it a little? That's all."

"Ok. How about if we meet in front of the hotel in about twenty minutes? I need to call the school and make sure the little devils haven't completely destroyed the place."

"Sounds like a plan."

Taking sex and the possibility of a relationship out of the equation took all the pressure off for Jerry. There was no objective or endgame. Not to say that he wouldn't have enjoyed a little nookie with this attractive and down-to-earth vegan woman. She was, in fact, Jerry's kind of girl. But a clear boundary had been established. The rules of engagement were clear. And conversation seemed to come so easily for them, and conversation would be all that mattered this afternoon. This would be nice, maybe even sublime, if sublime was possible without getting into this woman's panties. And what kind of panties did Joanie have? Probably all-cotton bikini briefs. Probably pink or flowery. They probably ran just below her hips — her unmistakably female hips with a nice little waggle.

Jerry had never had sex with a married woman. A few opportunities had come his way, but when it came down to it, he could never get over the fact that he'd be making some poor soul out there a cuckold. Even if the guy was a jerk, even if the husband himself had been unfaithful, poking his wife would be just plain wrong. It would give Jerry bad karma. And how much it would suck to be a husband whose wife went down on another guy? And what does that say about the wife? She'd probably have some intractable STD that remains asymptomatic for weeks until one morning you wake up and there's barnacles growing all over your balls. That would be Jerry's luck.

• • • •

Joanie and Jerry walked among the festival's arts and crafts exhibits talking about the perfect weather — how unusually clear and dry it was for Portland — and laughed and joked about whoopee cushions and butt cracks. In fact, they took notice of a few more exposed rear ends at the festival, including the particularly large one of the beefy pedal-steel guitarist bending over on the music stage. Jerry referred to it as "a fault line." Then there was the large-bootied woman selling jade jewelry who bent over to pet someone's dog. "That there's a crevasse. I think we've lost a few rock climbers in there," Jerry whispered into Joanie's ear. Inspired by the witticisms, she later dubbed Portland "Butt Crack City."

They came across a young woman with a baby in her lap selling friendship bracelets for three dollars from a small table. Wearing a flowered yellow sundress and her long blonde hair in a braided ponytail, she looked like a child herself, barely sixteen or seventeen. As Joanie looked at the bracelets, the baby stared with its mouth agape at Jerry. As Jerry smiled, the baby began to smile back.

"Hey, let's buy a couple of these as mementos of our trip," Joanie said turning to Jerry. "And we're friends, right?"

"Sure," Jerry answered.

"Well, pick one out that matches your wardrobe. Those green and blue ones are nice."

As he looked at the different bracelets, the baby continued to check him out. Jerry wondered about the little child. Was there a father in the picture? Was the mom earning enough money to support it? What a miraculous little life. How scary to be responsible for it. Yes, the blue and green bracelet was the best choice. If nothing else it was the most masculine.

"So what happens when I take a shower?" Jerry asked as Joanie tied it on his wrist. "Will it come off?"

"No, it is on there forever. You're locked in there, Zuckerman." After she finished tying his bracelet on his wrist, she handed him hers, which was brighter than his, made of twisting strands of purple and pink. "Now you tie mine. Actually, I think I left enough room so you can slide it off before taking a shower. Try to leave room so I can slide mine off, too."

A few minutes later, as Joanie was looking at the bottom of a piece of Native American pottery, she said, "You know, in a village somewhere in

Africa, I think it's called Bunga Bunga, these bracelets mean that our karma is forever linked." She put the bowl down and looked intently at Jerry. "So that means if you do something awful, it's bad for both our karmas. But if you do something good, it's good for both our karmas. So now you really need to behave."

"Really?" Jerry said, looking dismayed at the bracelet, taken aback by the implications of it.

Joanie looked at him for a moment, expressionless. Then she smiled. "Nah, I'm just shitting you! You are *so* gullible!"

"Fucker," he said, nudging her shoulder, embarrassed that he'd fallen for her little joke.

The sun reflected off the quiescent Willamette River more and more spectacularly as the afternoon wore on. Later in the day, Joanie and Jerry sat on the grass just a few yards from the river listening to a jazz trio play ballads. The combo was lead by a trumpet player who Jerry said sounded like Chet Baker.

"That sound is so mellowing," he said. "It makes me feel like I'm on opium. It reminds me of summer evenings back in Cleveland when I was a kid. We used to just hang out on the front steps of somebody's house and talk. Maybe we'd flip baseball cards or set off some firecrackers. Ok, setting off fireworks wasn't so relaxing, but we had no concept of time. Summers seemed to have no end."

Joanie smiled. "I know what you mean. Then we grew up, and, well, life happens, and here we are." She looked over at the sun setting behind a building, then at her watch. "I really need to get back for the dinner, Jerry. It's starting soon. I paid thirty bucks for it. And I'd better hear 'what's-his-name' speak. The church ladies are going to want to hear all about his talk. You know he's the cattle farmer turned vegan." She looked at Jerry apologetically.

Jerry's heart sunk a little, but he was careful not show it. "No problem.

Of course, I understand. I passed on the dinner. My boss, El Cheapo, didn't want to spring for it. And I've been to a zillion of them anyway. But this afternoon was really a lot of fun."

Joanie seemed flustered. She got up quickly. "I can't tell you the last time I had such a great time. I don't know, you're really a great guy, Jerry." She paused and looked at him as if she needed some kind of help, but she herself didn't know what help that might be. "Anyway, maybe we can catch up tomorrow."

Jerry decided not to walk back with her. He felt awkward about the abruptness of her departure and didn't want to make her think he was latching on. "Sounds good. Enjoy the dinner." He watched her walk up the grassy slope out of the park, wondering if he'd ever see her again.

He had to give another presentation the next day and felt jet-lagged, so maybe this was for the best. The afternoon had gone by in an instant. It had been wonderful. He tried to look at his few hours with Joanie as just a good time, nothing more. Then he imagined her going home to a husband with a chiseled, manly face and big biceps, a really cool tattoo on one of them, and, of course, a Yankees cap. Those fucking sell-out Yankees. They always win.

• • • •

Jerry's three o'clock presentation, a repeat of the same shtick he'd given the previous morning, was standing room only. He estimated there to be a crowd of at least seventy-five, and people kept coming in, even several minutes after he started. Afternoon sessions usually drew fewer people, so Jerry was both pleased and perplexed. Maybe he had less competition from other speakers than he had yesterday. Regardless, he felt energized, even buoyant. While big audiences gave him jitters, he always performed better in front of large crowds once he got started.

As he reached his penultimate slide, the hoarder with all her bags in tow slid into the front row. She had on the same royal-blue sweat pants, but a different shirt, dark green. How bizarre. What the fuck was she going to ask him this time? Maybe now she wants to piss on her vegetables. If that was the case, he'd tell her, "Sounds good to me. Go for it." But as inexplicably as she had arrived, she left as Jerry finished.

A few people made their way up to the front to talk to him. As he answered their questions and listened to their comments, the room cleared out quickly. Within a couple of minutes, everyone was gone except for Joanie standing in the back of the room. Dressed in denim shorts and a sleeveless t-shirt, she looked like an embarrassed child, who had come to ask forgiveness for some misdeed — like leaving the house for several hours without telling her parents.

But Jerry wasn't looking for any apologies or explanations. Joanie hadn't done anything wrong; she had been open and honest. They had had a fun afternoon as friends. That was it. Last night, he had decided to try and forget about her, and instead, focus on the conference and his presentation that afternoon. But now he was excited to see her again.

"You really know how to pack'em in there, Zuckerman," she said after making her way up to the podium where Jerry stood. She looked even more beautiful than yesterday — had she done something different with her hair? — but at the same time, was more uncomfortable. She couldn't keep her hands or feet still.

"I have to say, I was surprised by how many people showed up, especially this late in the day. No complaints here. I hate doing these things for just ten people. It's like throwing a party and no one shows."

"Listen," Joanie said, relieved to be cutting to the chase. "I was wondering if you were around for dinner tonight. I found an outdoor cafe down the street with some vegan Middle Eastern options. Maybe we can walk around some more. I think the festival is still going on."

"That would be great. Let's meet at six in front of the hotel."

"Actually, if you aren't doing anything, how about if we go for a walk now, while it's still warm? It's just so nice out."

"OK. Let me just go back to my room and change."

Joanie Sanders always had a hard time holding back her feelings. It's what drew people to her, and at the same time, scared them away. While it never had been a conscious decision, her and her husband's hectic lives never left much opportunity for Joanie to be her vulnerable and playful self. Though she cherished her motherly role for her special-needs students, she missed being the little girl she had never wanted to stop being — to joke around, to be taken care of, and perhaps most important, to live in the moment. And in just a few hours with Jerry Zuckerman, sometimes a boy himself, she felt again what it was like to be that little kid.

They stood shoulder to shoulder, looking out over the rippling Willamette for more than an hour with the sounds from the festival, more lively than the day before, coming from grassy hill behind them — someone on the stage pumping out a bluesy riff on a harmonica, the whirring fan from the kids' moon bounce, the incessant barking of a little dog spooked by the crowd of humans milling about.

When Jerry suggested they start heading over to the cafe, Joanie decided she couldn't hold back any longer. "OK. But I have to say something. This is going to sound weird Jerry, but I've never felt like this before. Well, at least not that I can remember. I mean with you. Yesterday was just so much fun. It was incredible. I feel like I've known you forever." She hesitated, pulling up a strap on the lavender top that had fallen down her arm. "I know I sound a little crazy, but I am not sure what's happening."

For Jerry, the chemistry was obvious. Yes, they were having a great time together. And the parameters of their relationship — just friends — meant there were no expectations. But he realized for Joanie, their short platonic thing together had led her to something more. In a way it was flattering for him, that he was having such a strong romantic effect on this woman. On the other hand, he knew that it was probably as much about the result of her having being married for several years. The passion fades. Familiarity breeds boredom. He always believed that the people who made their long-term relationships work did so out of co-dependence. The wife deals with her low self-esteem by bitching at her husband, and for the husband, her bitching is affirmation that he exists, that he matters. Their dysfunctional yin-yang takes precedence over their otherwise humdrum, inconsequential lives. And kids are just another seal on the deal.

Jerry briefly fantasized about spending the last two days together in Portland back at the hotel in fornicative bliss. Just fucking. Being fucked. Ordering room service. Fucking some more. But then what? He didn't want to get in the middle of her apparently "happy" marriage.

"Look," he said to Joanie. "You're so fun and I might add, pretty cute. I really enjoy being with you. But you're married. And happily, right?"

"I thought so," she answered, looking anguished.

"Well, I am the last guy you want to take any risks with. I mean, I'm not long-term relationship material. I get scared. I get bored. I made one attempt at marriage and didn't even make it to the altar. If you go back to Albany and decide your marriage with 'what's-his-name'."

"Dan."

"...with Dan isn't working, well, I'd love to see you again. But right now, you're married, you live in Albany, I'm in DC. It would just be so messy."

Joanie shook her head and looked out over the river. She started tearing up. As Jerry put his arm around her, she rested her head on his shoulder. Then she looked up at him. "Where the fuck did you come from Jerry Zuckerman, you vegan environmental geek-boy from DC?" Then she pushed him lightly. "You're such a bastard."

Jerry shrugged his shoulders. "Hey, I just came to Butt Crack City to help save the animals. And besides, you came up to me."

Joanie pushed her finger into his chest. "Yeah, but I was

minding my own business when you came over and made the move on my French fries."

"Actually, the fries hadn't quite arrived when I came to your table."

"Yeah, but you knew food was coming. You made a preemptive strike."

"What can I say? I have good instincts. And how often does a guy come across an attractive vegan woman sitting alone in a bar?"

"Well, I was looking for Mr. Vegan Goodbar."

Joanie and Jerry were inseparable for the next day and a half. They completely blew off the conference on Sunday and spent most of the day walking by the river and hanging out at the festival. On Saturday and Sunday nights, they slept side-by-side together, though fully clothed, in Joanie's hotel room. Joanie kept commenting on how well they spooned together, how they seemed like a perfect fit. For Jerry, yes, it was nice, but the physical intimacy left him in a constant state of rock-hard arousal. He felt like he was bursting at the seams. At one point, he slid his hand into her shorts and caressed her from behind, but never reaching in front, crossing into forbidden territory — not that Joanie forbade it. Rather, it was Jerry who was reluctant to cross that line, to lead Joanie down the path of infidelity. While he wondered how he would deal with having slept with a married woman, he was more concerned about Joanie's reaction to being unfaithful. Sure, she might go for it in the heat of the moment, but she was so sensitive and honest. He worried that her cheating would later eat her alive. Eventually she'd confess to her husband, and from there, her life would implode.

Jerry would be the first to leave Portland. His flight was departing at eleven on Monday morning. Joanie wasn't leaving until Tuesday morning. On Sunday night, the reality of their imminent separation began creating a sense of urgency to figure out how to move forward, together or apart. As they lay in bed on their backs, Joanie turned to Jerry, putting a hand on his arm. Mocking enthusiasm, she said, "Maybe I could leave Dan, get half his money in the divorce settlement, and then we could open a vegan petting zoo for both kids and adults. I could buy a couple of acres. We could have a vegan cafe. Teach everyone about eating vegan and protecting animal rights. Hey, that would be great!" She paused for a moment, but maintained her mischievous expression of delight. "Dan, that fucker, is such a meat-eater. He invites his buddies over and grills steaks and burgers right in front of me. He completely disses the vegetarian thing. If I opened a vegan petting zoo with his money, it would give him a coronary!"

"There's two problems with that strategy," Jerry said while looking out the window. "First, Dan will not give you a nickel if you leave him because you're cheating on him, and two, I'm allergic to animals. I mean really allergic."

"Wow, sorry to hear that. Well, maybe we could put you in a bubble and you could be a side show. Like the grown-up Bubble Boy. The Bubble Man! The Bubble Guy! Yeah, Bubba the Bubble Guy! You could just sit there and drink beer and watch TV. Sort of like a vegan freak show."

Jerry pushed Joanie on her back, and mounted her, holding her arms down. "You are so brilliant. That is what I am going to miss most about you. Your incredible mind," he said, holding his face in front of hers. Then for the first time he kissed her on the lips, relishing their softness. Surprised and scared by his own impulsiveness, he pulled away after only a few seconds.

"That was nice. I could get used to that," Joanie said, hoping he'd kiss her again.

But Jerry didn't respond. He took a deep breath and lay there looking at the ceiling. Doubt was getting the better of him. What were they doing in this odd little unconsummated affair? There was no future in it. Even if Joanie decided to leave Dan, she and Jerry lived hundreds of miles apart. How would they see each other on a regular basis? And they hardly new each other having spent only a weekend together. Was there any chance that their relationship would work? Not really.

So Jerry made a compromise with himself. He would spend this last night with Joanie and make it a point to remember everything he could about her. The bounty of her hair. The loss and innocence in her smile. Sharing fries in the bar while they conspired to skip the conference for the afternoon. The moment he saw her waiting to reunite with him after his presentation the next day. And now they had the delight and agony of being together alone, but their time running out. But this would have to be enough — this little romantic drama — and maybe not trying to make more of it would enable it to retain its magic. If they took it much further, they'd likely burn and crash like Icarus. Without taking it further, he'd always have the memory — the taste of it always on the tip of his tongue.

Jerry left hastily in the morning. He wasn't rude — he just couldn't stomach lingering for too long, which would inevitably have led to an emotional goodbye. "Joanie, this has been wonderful, but I need to get upstairs and pack and get to the airport," he said as he put on his shoes. Still groggy, Joanie sat up in bed and watched him for a few seconds. Then she got up and went into the bathroom, after telling him that she'd be right back.

A couple of minutes later, they stood in the doorway of her hotel room, both at a loss for words. Joanie began to cry. Jerry, shaking his head, began to tear up himself. He took her hand and kissed her on the lips. Looking into her reddened eyes, he said, "You're so beautiful, Joanie Sanders." Then he gave her another kiss, turned away, and went to the elevator.

• • • •

As the taxi left the airport and headed back downtown, Pete kept glancing into his rearview mirror looking at Jerry, who was intently telling his story about Joanie. Pete thought Jerry's predicament was right up his alley; Pete knew all about these trysts, affairs, flings, whatever you want to call them. He often made the point that there were more of these "indiscretions" than there were marriages or long-term relationships. It's human nature to stray and be lured by what's forbidden or taboo. We all want what we can't or shouldn't have.

"So now miraculously, I'm heading back to the hotel where she'll be. Her flight doesn't leave until tomorrow," Jerry said as Pete nodded. "I can't wait to see her again. I can't believe this is happening."

Pete picked up a toothpick from a compartment in the console next to his seat and then pointed it at Jerry's image in the rearview mirror. "When you get back there, you should just fuck her. *That's* what you should do." Pete put the toothpick in his mouth. "Happily married? Yeah, whatever. If not you, it will be some other joe at some point. You both want it. That's the bottom line."

Jerry was initially put off by the brashness of Pete's remark. And this guy had been a psychotherapist? He must have gotten his counseling certification online or through some infomercial on TV. No wonder he couldn't stay married.

But after considering the advice for a few moments, Jerry started thinking that maybe Pete was right, and he had completely over-analyzed the situation. Maybe he and Joanie should have sex — make the most of their remaining time together, really go for it — and then it would be over. They could go back to their lives. And who knows what's really happening in her relationship? Maybe Dan had cheated on Joanie. Maybe he picked up hookers or was banging his secretary. Who knows? Maybe there's a little justice in Joanie being unfaithful. He's an insensitive carnivorous Yankees fan. He must be a fucking jerk.

Jerry felt numb as walked back into the hotel. The weekend had worn him out, but at the same time, the anticipation of seeing Joanie again gave him renewed energy. It was a gift. Sex or not, he wanted to stroll along the Willamette with her again and then lie beside her in the evening. And even though he was the reason for her turmoil, he wanted to comfort her, reassure her, tell her everything would be ok regardless of what happened between them. Somehow, this reunion would make things better, easier.

"It's your favorite vegan boomerang. You can toss me out, but I always come right back," he would say when Joanie came to the door. But several seconds passed after he knocked. A few moments after knocking a second time and getting no response, Jerry felt like the earth's gravitational force was causing all his blood to drain to his legs. The stillness on the other side of the door took the wind out of him. Before he called the front desk on the house phone at the end of the hall, he knew she was gone. It made sense for her to leave. Why stay in Portland another day alone in a hotel room, especially the room where they had been together? It made sense for her to get back to her students and Dan and put this fiasco behind her as quickly as she could. It was over.

After Jerry checked into a room, he sat on the bed for a few minutes at a loss for what to do next. He realized that Joanie's taxi to the airport had probably passed him and Pete on the freeway. For a split second, they had been just a few feet from one another, but heading in completely opposite directions. How lucky he had been in the first place that she came up to him after his presentation, and that he went up to her in the bar a couple of hours later. That would have to be enough.

With no plan for the afternoon except to not be alone in his room, Jerry took a shower, changed into jeans and a t-shirt, and headed down near the river to walk around. It was another perfectly clear day with only a few jet streams crisscrossing the deep-blue sky. Remarkably, workers had already disassembled and loaded up all of the festival tents. There was no trace of the bounce house or music stage. Just a few portable johns and garbage cans remained.

Jerry noticed a photo of a beagle taped to a telephone pole at the crest of the hill — the same hill that Joanie had walked up after hastily leaving him that first night. The dog was plump, and grey around the eyebrows and muzzle. It looked like it was sniffing out a treat being held by someone out of the range of the camera. The sign read, "LOST BEAGLE. ANSWERS TO LIZZIE. HARD OF HEARING. FRIENDLY." How sad — an old lost beagle wandering the streets of Portland. How the hell did this sweet, innocent animal lose its way?

Jerry sat up against the pole and looked out over the Willamette. What a weekend. But he felt like he was now where he needed to be: present, alone, and unfound.

Josie

Marty never called all-staff meetings. Jerry could remember only one such gathering during his twelve-year tenure at the Vegetarian Action Committee, and it had been convened to announce the death of a board member on the West Coast who no one on staff except Marty had ever known or seen. The founder and executive director of the Committee tried to maintain control by not sharing information — even information about the nonprofit's volunteer leadership. Regardless, because the staff never grew beyond ten employees, all of whom worked under the same roof, everyone knew most of the Committee's business anyway. It was difficult to keep anything confidential.

But the source of most of the Committee's revenues had remained a complete mystery. Marty kept the books himself and revealed nothing about them. While some money came from membership dues, magazine subscriptions, and occasional direct gifts, more than two-thirds of the Committee's annual income, six hundred thousand dollars, came through an annuity from a foundation called EarthOne — or at least that was the name of the entity as it appeared on IRS 990 forms published openly on the Internet. As much as staff and nosy members of competing veg organizations tried, no one could ever figure out who or what EarthOne was, though they knew that he, she, or it was critical to the daily operations of the Committee. If anyone ever asked Marty about EarthOne, he said it was an anonymous donor, end of story. He'd always grin after a question he didn't want to answer, like those about EarthOne or the inner workings of the Committee. But it wasn't a friendly or an apologetic smile. Rather it was the kind of off-kilter expression that a serial killer might make before disemboweling his victim.

With a scruffy beard and out-of-control mop of mostly grey hair, Marty always appeared haggard. He dressed in Wrangler jeans, flannel shirts, and work boots. He looked as if he was prepared to go picking strawberries with migrant farm-workers. Marty could never be accused of coasting or slacking off — he worked twelve-hour days and often weekends — but continual worry got the better of him. He obsessed about everything from a font in a brochure to the placement of a lock on the Committee's bathroom door.

Staff knew something was wrong a few days before Marty sent out the e-mail announcing the meeting. Instead of his usual M.O. of critiquing and tweaking everyone's work, he spent the better part of the week in his office with the door closed. The few times he did emerge, he looked distraught. Rumors swirled among the staff, and most were directed at his health. He had no significant other and few family members, so if something was wrong, it probably had to do with him.

But the issue was money, not the "Marty is dying" theory that had gained traction around the office. And it was a financial problem that was completely unexpected and inevitably catastrophic. EarthOne pulled the plug on its support. No one, including Marty, saw it coming, and he seemed in disbelief as he stood in front of his staff in the reception area, the largest room in the office, on a mid-August afternoon.

Marty couldn't look at the faces of his employees. Instead, he stared at his feet. Then the phone on the reception desk behind him rang, breaking the tension. After it stopped ringing, he cleared his throat. "The Vegetarian Action Committee has just taken a big financial blow," he said fixating on the framed image of the "VAC" logo on the back wall of the room. "Our largest donor — a private, anonymous donor — is no longer on board with us. And without their support, we can't survive. I mean, they account for more than half of our income. The math is pretty simple."

Relieved at the moment to finally get the news out, Marty sat down on the reception desk and looked at his employees to see their reaction. Everyone else in the room was stunned into silence. No one had imagined that the Committee would be shutting its doors. Several small vegetarian groups had come and gone over the years, but the Committee, with Marty at the helm, had been a stalwart for nearly three decades. It seemed like it would go on forever.

Marty continued. "The only hope I saw was for us to merge with another group, so I made some calls. But no one was interested. Everybody's cutting back because of the economy. So, with what we have in the bank, we'll be able to get the next issue of the magazine out and stay open through most of October. We can keep everyone on the payroll until then. No problem if anyone wants to leave early."

After pausing again to see if anyone had anything to say, Marty said, "Any questions?"

Joe, the webmaster, asked if there would be an extension of health insurance beyond October.

"I'm looking into that now," Marty answered. "I'll send out a note when I figure out what the options are." He paused again to see if anyone else had anything to say. The employees looked at each other, but no one spoke. "OK. You know where to find me if there's anything you want to talk about." Marty got up off the desk and walked back to his office.

Jerry's immediate reaction was disappointment and anger at Marty. After all these years, the guy couldn't express any emotion or appreciation to all the employees who worked their asses off for near-minimum wages? And the Vegetarian Action Committee was his baby for Christ's sake! He had spent most of his life running the organization. And now, just like that, it was shutting down?

In the coming days, panic set in for Jerry. He woke up every morning feeling anxious, because he didn't have much in the way of prospects for life after the Committee. Every new day was a day closer to unemployment. He'd been out of technology sales for too long to easily move back into it. Most of the computer networking products he'd been trained on had become quaint relics on display at the Smithsonian. Furthermore, he had no desire to move back into any kind of sales — technology or otherwise — and spend his time cold calling and knocking on doors, working to maximize some company's stock price. And while he found his vegetarian education and advocacy work rewarding, most veg groups were downsizing, as Marty had pointed out. Now in his forties, any kind of major career change would be a formidable undertaking. And going back to school would mean taking on a lot of debt at a time when he should start saving for retirement.

Jerry relaxed more in the evenings; he was better able to imagine and fantasize about his future when the sun went down. Surfing around the Internet late into the night, he perused Web sites recruiting people to teach English in Korea and China. He found sites for various farms — both in the U.S. and abroad — which needed people who would work for room and board. Working the fields seemed like a fulfilling existential pursuit — get his hands dirty, eat the food he grew, sleep with horny hippie chicks with hairy legs and armpits. To his surprise, he also found thriving communes operating all over the United States. Maybe he'd join one of those and weave baskets, smoke dope, and sleep with horny hippie chicks with hairy legs and armpits. Maybe he'd join the Peace Corps and help starving kids in Africa. Maybe now was the time he did something truly bold and life-changing.

But after a night of fantastical ideas whirling around in his head, he would wake up wondering what the hell he had been thinking. There's no way he'd last a week in any of those remote, primitive locales without running water, toilet paper, air conditioning, or Starbucks. There would be no place to get an emergency condom or catch a Coen Brothers movie. And except for a few months with his ex-fiancée, Missy, he hadn't lived with anyone for the last twenty years. He could barely tolerate a weekend out-of-town guest in his own apartment. Clearly, a radical life change was neither prudent nor feasible at this stage of the game.

Two weeks after Marty's announcement, while having coffee after work, Suzy told Jerry that she'd landed a job as a teaching assistant at the Montessori school where he had presented to the students and inadvertently helped inspire one of the fourth graders, Francesca, to go vegetarian. "I hope you don't mind that I didn't tell you I was interviewing there. I was afraid I'd jinx it," she said. "I don't know, I really like working with kids, and Mrs. Kumar was so cool about Francesca's parents freaking out about her going veg. I heard they had an opening, so I called her up. The job doesn't pay very well, but I can afford it, at least for a while. Honestly, I never thought I'd get it. There are so many real teachers out of work right now."

"Good for you," Jerry said. "Really. It is tough out there. I think you should take whatever you can get, and if you think you'll enjoy it, all the better. Frankly, I have no idea what the hell I'm going to do. I'm bumming out big time."

"I know, Jerr, I know. No one is finding much. Everyone is upset. Have you talked with Marty at all? He is well connected. If there's anything out there, he'd know about it."

"You're right, but I feel desperate going to him. He can be such an asshole when you ask him a favor."

"True, but in two months, you'll never have to deal with him again, except maybe for a reference."

"Good point," Jerry said, recognizing he wasn't in a position to be too proud or picky.

As he left the cafe with Suzy, he remembered how a strange twist of fate twelve years ago at the county fair had ultimately brought him to the Vegetarian Action Committee. Petting that soon-to-be slaughtered lamb. Taking the vegetarian brochure from Suzy at the entrance gate of the fair.

And then being a detained "accomplice" in that vegan geek's brawl with the biker. Who knew where his next life-changing opportunity might come from? As deliberate as he as felt he needed to be in planning his next move, he knew he couldn't necessarily predict or force his fate.

The next day, his conversation with Marty seemingly went nowhere. Marty told him he should get back into computer sales, dismissing Jerry's argument that he'd been out of the business too long. "But there's good money in it. And everybody needs a computer," Marty insisted. "You went to college for it, right? A computer is a computer. Selling is selling. You're a smart guy."

"But Marty, even if I could jump right back into it, it isn't what I want to do," Jerry countered. "Remember when I joined the Committee and I told you I had burned out on selling technology and was looking for something more meaningful?"

"I'll tell you, Jerry. Making money would be pretty meaningful to me right now."

"Yeah, Marty, but you did a lot of good for many, many years. The Committee even helped inspire me to give up meat."

The remark bounced right off Marty. It was the most complimentary thing Jerry had ever said to him, yet he was unable to even acknowledge it. Marty just turned around without saying a word and walked back to his office.

A few minutes later, Jerry received an e-mail from Marty that had links from an employment listserv to various jobs in the vegetarian and animal-rights community. One by one, Jerry went through them. Most were for positions in vegetarian-only restaurants — hosts, servers, cooks — and many were on the West Coast. The last link led to a description that read: "Experienced fundraiser needed for farm animal sanctuary near Missoula, Montana. Send résumé and cover letter to g.antonizzi-silverman@safas.org." Interesting — an Italian-Jew saving animals in the hinterlands. There was something intriguing, perhaps familiar about the job listing, but Jerry couldn't put his finger on why.

Before he drifted off to sleep that night — with the events of the day randomly passing through what remained of his consciousness — Jerry realized why that blurb about the animal sanctuary struck a chord. It was the name Antonizzi. He recognized it. Gail Antonizzi was that smart, cute girl who befriended him in sixth grade. The girl he kind of had a crush on. The girl who proclaimed her vegetarianism at Irv's Sandwich Shop. But the e-mail user name was "g.antonizzi-silverman." At first, it didn't seem plausible to Jerry that she married a Jewish guy, moved to Montana, and started an animal sanctuary. But the more he thought about it, the more possible he thought it could be. She did like advocating for underdogs. And there were lots of Jewish guys in Cleveland Heights — he could see her having hooked up with one. Though moving to Montana did seem like a stretch. But then again, it would be a good place for the animals.

He couldn't contain his curiosity, so he got out of bed, turned on his computer, and began to search the Internet. In a few minutes, he found the homepage for Sunny Acres Farm Animal Sanctuary in Montana, clicked on the About Us tab, and there was a photo of Gail Antonizzi-Silverman, Executive Director, smiling earnestly as she brushed a cow. There was no mistaking her big brown eyes and long brunette ponytail. Sure, Gail had grayed a bit and filled out a little since sixth grade — no surprise after thirty years — but she appeared vital and happy.

• • • •

As the prop plane wended its way toward Missoula over rugged hills and snow-capped mountains, Jerry remembered reading that the city had been built on the bed of what had once been a glacial lake. The water must have looked beautiful on a crisp, clear autumn day like today. But now, the expansive Missoula Valley, at the convergence of five mountain ranges, was smattered with small communities, farms, and fall colors. Even with man's inhabitance — his passion for destruction and construction — it still looked pristine.

Jerry began feeling apprehensive about seeing Gail again. Hell, they were sixth graders the last time they saw each other. They were completely different people now. Grown up, worn around the edges, and a little more jaded and set in their ways. And he was visiting for almost two weeks. What if they didn't get along? In one of her e-mails, she mentioned her divorce and still being in "start-up mode" with the sanctuary. Hopefully, he wasn't about to plop himself into the middle of a crisis. But Jerry also looked forward to letting go of his life in DC for a while and his own troubles. He needed space and distance. And as the plane made its final approach toward the humble oasis in the Northern Rockies, he felt he'd gain perspective there.

When Jerry walked into the baggage claim area and saw Gail in faded jeans with knee patches and a brown flannel jacket, it was clear she had acclimated well to her new life in Montana. She had on a little fresh make-up, but otherwise looked like a woman who worked the land, and gladly so.

"I can't believe you're here, Jerry," she said as they embraced. "Who knew that we'd reunite in Montana of all places after all these years?"

"And as two crazy vegans at that! You look great, Gail. You look happy."

"I think I am, Jerry. I think I am. I had a tough go of it for a while after my marriage went kaplooie, but the animals keep me busy."

Within ten minutes, they were leaving the desolate airport parking lot in Gail's pick-up truck. "Hey, if it is ok with you, let's stop at Starbucks. I come to town about three or four days a week and always make it a point to stop there. Keeps me connected to city life."

"I'd love it, Gail. I'm there twice a day back in DC. I actually live two blocks from one."

"Wow. I'm jealous. I do miss being in a city sometimes, but since the ranch is about an hour from town, I can come in almost any time, if I need something or want to go out for dinner or a movie."

"So why exactly did you choose Montana?" Jerry asked. "Not there's anything wrong out here — it's so beautiful. I love the mountains all around. It's incredible."

"Well, Jerome," she said smiling at him, "I really got lucky, at least I think I did. When I knew I wanted to start a sanctuary, I was open to just about anywhere in the country, though the East and West Coast properties were pricey for me. Anyway, after a few months of searching, I found a retiring couple out here, who had a sixty-acre ranch and twenty-seven dairy cows. They were having a tough time selling the property, so it seemed like a good fit. And, they were just days away from foreclosure. So I got a good deal and saved a lot of animals in the process. The cows are my girls — they're wonderful."

"But I read on your Web site you've rescued more animals — some pigs and sheep?"

"Yeah. For the first year, year and a half, I wanted to make sure I could handle the cows, but I did take in a few other animals if someone came to me with them. I wouldn't turn them away. With what I got from my ex, I can afford what I'm doing now. But to expand much more, I need to raise more money. That's why I want someone to help with fundraising."

"Sorry about the divorce, Gail. That must have been hard."

"Yeah, we'll talk. I'll spare you the gory details for now."

After stopping for coffee, they headed south through the valley on Highway 93. Gail noticed that Jerry was taken by the idyllic backdrop. She pointed out the Bitterroot Mountains, many covered in thick pine, to their left, and the weather-worn Sapphire range to the right. It was the clearest sky Jerry had seen in a long time. Occasional puffy clouds moved over the valley from west to east. Gail lamented the plethora of fishermen and hunters that were drawn to the region, but for the most part, she said, it was a good place for wildlife, including deer, elk, even an occasional bear, and lots of fish and birds.

"This isn't Cleveland Heights," she said, chuckling. "Sometimes I wake up in the morning, and I can't believe I'm here, even after a year and a half.

At times it seems like a fantasy. Other times it seems like a nightmare. But over the past few months, my emotions have leveled off. My family and friends back home still think I lost it." Gail paused as she accelerated around a couple of slow-moving tractor trailers, then she glanced over at Jerry. "I guess I did lose it. But it feels right to be here. On the land. With my girls. I sure don't want to go back to Cleveland."

"But don't you get lonely out here?" Jerry asked. "I mean, no friends, no family. You live alone."

"Well, I have people on the property every day. Volunteers. A couple of part-time hands. A few kids from the college work here for class credits. They love it. You'll be sharing the cabin with a couple of them later in the week. Don't worry — you'll have separate sleeping areas. Like I said, you're welcome to stay in the house with me, I have three bedrooms, but I understand your allergies to the cats. They're mostly outside or in the barn, but we'll see how you feel."

Jerry admired Gail for taking the chance to come out to Montana and start over. It took incredible courage. He remembered her being a bold and determined kid in sixth grade, so it wasn't a complete surprise that she made this move. Back in school, she didn't care what anyone else thought. She did what she felt was right, especially when it came to sticking up for others who were disenfranchised or just a little different. She believed that everyone deserved a chance to be on a team or get a little help with their homework. Everyone deserved to belong. And now she was sticking up for the animals.

"The ranch is just a couple of miles down the road," Gail said as she made a left turn off the highway. "I know on paper it's a sanctuary, but I usually just call it the ranch, because that's what it feels like. You know, there's a lot of hay, a lot of cow shit, fences, barns. It's a ranch with permanent residents."

Gail purposely didn't say anything as she pulled the truck up the driveway to the small but modern lodge home that fronted the property. She was curious how Jerry would react on his own to seeing the sanctuary for the first time. Besides her daughter, Eve, who came out for a week over the summer before starting her freshman year at the University of California, San Francisco, no one else from out of town had visited. Adopted from China as an infant, Eve didn't take well to ranch life. Like many kids her age growing up in the suburbs, she was into boys, cell phones, and computers. She wanted to hang out with her friends — not retired dairy cows in the middle of Montana. But Gail hoped that Jerry would appreciate the new life that she had created for herself. After eighteen months, it really began to feel like hers. The roots had taken hold. She was proud of her animals and the comfortable home she had given them. And it was becoming her home, too.

The house, along with a nearby cabin, two barns, and a big corral, stood atop a gently sloping pasture. A half-dozen broad trees full of golden leaves provided shade nearby. A young man in a baseball cap holding a shovel waved from the corral. "Hey Joey," yelled Gail, waving back. "He's one of my part-time hands," she said as they walked toward the corral. "Lots of guys wanted to work for the new single woman. Heh, heh. He's got some type of learning disability. At least that's what his parents told me. Dropped out of school. But he was the most gentle with the animals. Loves the work."

"You're the same girl I knew at Taylor Elementary School," Jerry said. "Always giving the underdog a chance."

Gail smiled and shrugged her shoulders. "I guess, but I do have bigger boobs now."

"Do you?" Jerry said, mocking surprise.

"You're damn right I do!" Gail shouted back. "I also have a shotgun under my bed. Girl's got to take care of herself out here."

"Really?"

"Don't worry. I went to the shooting range to learn how to use it."

Jerry stopped walking. "So let me get this straight," he said. "You're a packing single vegan woman with large boobs, nonetheless living alone in the middle of Montana."

"We're actually in Western Montana," Gail said pointing her finger at Jerry.

"Oh. Excuse me. I stand corrected."

When they reached the corral, Gail introduced Jerry to Joey, and then to two sheep, Daisy and Pedro, which had sauntered over to see if there were any treats to be had. As she scratched one of the animals under its neck, Gail said that she got Daisy when some girl in an afterschool agricultural program learned that the beloved friend she was caring for was eventually headed for slaughter. Word spread among the kids that Sunny Acres would take the animals, and that was how Pedro came to the sanctuary.

"The families bought the animals and then brought them here. I might get more of their refugees next year, but I don't want to be their dumping ground. Then again, I would be saving the animals. And educating kids would be great. That's one of my goals, but that takes people and money — another reason for fundraising."

Gail pointed back to one of the barns. "That's where the pigs are right now, Bonnie and Clyde. Yeah, a farm was shutting down last year, and they asked me to take them. I have room for more small animals and will take them in if asked. I'm sure I will be at some point. I would like some chickens and goats, too."

Jerry gazed out over the bucolic landscape — the pasture filled with large, round hay bales, the distant mountains, a few stray clouds. A light, invigorating breeze came in from the north. He could see what appeared to be Gail's cows off in the distance. The herd was looking back toward the sanctuary to see what the action was all about. "Do you get used to looking at this scenery everyday?" he asked Gail. "It's incredible."

"I guess I am used to it. It will never be like seeing it for the first time," she answered, scratching the head of the other sheep. "But I guess now I look at it as my home."

"Not a bad place to call home."

Gail smiled back and nodded. Having a visitor, especially an old friend, and a vegan, a person who loved the animals, was exactly what she needed after being in Montana without any family. She was glad to see him appreciating the sanctuary. She had been concerned about his motives for coming out. A romantic fling with a guy who lived two thousand miles away was the last thing on her agenda, and she had hinted that fact in her e-mails to him. But his relief to be staying in the animal-free cabin was a relief to her. He couldn't be too much of a pervert if he wanted to bunk in separate quarters. He hadn't turned gay, had he?

As they walked over to the barns, Gail explained that the sanctuary was preparing for winter. Joey's responsibilities included keeping the corral and barns clean, managing the delivery and distribution of hay, and spreading manure. The cows had thinned out the pasture and would soon be eating hay until late spring. She had talked to some local farmers who agreed that getting the manure on the fields now was a good idea. Hopefully, it would help the pasture come in thick next year.

Her other employee, a handy, semi-retired guy named Gregg, took care of most of the equipment, the tractor, and inspecting and mending the fences. He had worked with the previous owners, and Gail agreed to take him on when she purchased the property. "The mechanical stuff does not come easy for me, but Gregg is patient and very willing to teach me some of the basics. Back in Cleveland, I could barely pump my own gas."

After walking back to the corral, Gail and Joey talked for a few minutes about where the next bales of hay should go when they arrived in a day or two. Then Joey shook Jerry's hand before leaving. "Nice to meet you, sir. I'll see you guys tomorrow," he said as he opened the gate to the corral. "Enjoy your lasagna dinner. Mrs. A's the best cook around."

“Yeah, I keep everyone well fed around here,” Gail said grinning sheepishly. “That’s my secret weapon. I hope you like lasagna. Joey insisted that I make it for you. I have to admit — it’s pretty damn good.”

“Sound’s great to me, Gail.”

Then she took Jerry’s hand and led him out of the corral, a few yards into the pasture. Looking out toward the herd that stood about one hundred yards away, she cupped her hands around her mouth and yelled, “Girrrrrrlllls! Come on girls! Come on! Come on now!” She took a few more steps into the field and called them again, “Come on girls! Come on!”

Several of the animals answered back, mooing nasally moos in acknowledgement. It was as if they were saying, “Ok, ok. We’re coming. Hold your horses.” And in short order, the entire herd had worked up to a slow trot toward Gail and Jerry. As they got closer, they broke into a gallop, their tails flopping back and forth. To Jerry, they were like a rush of puppies at dinnertime. They were magnificent creatures with hulking bodies and large intense eyes. Some were black and white Holsteins, others brown Jerseys. They continued to moo vociferously as they slowed to greet their human friends. A few came right up to Gail. “You are such beautiful girls, aren’t you?” she said as she vigorously rubbed one’s nose and neck. “Come on over Uncle Jerry and show the girls some love. Did you know he came all the way from Washington to see you?”

But Uncle Jerry was reaching in his pocket for a handkerchief to wipe tears from his eyes. He was surprised to be so moved by the grace of the animals. He had no idea they were capable of such affection, and it touched him at his vegan core.

“You ok, Jerr? Your allergies acting up?”

“No, I’m fine. Just got a little choked up. That was something else, Gail. The way they just ran over to you. Wow.”

“They’re my girls, Jerr. They’re my girls.”

Jerry walked up to one of the Holsteins and began rubbing her forehead. The cow unfurled its long tongue and licked his hand. Then she nudged Jerry's arm with her nose. The warm breath from the animal's big nostrils felt amazing to him; Jerry had never been so close with such a massive, friendly creature.

"That's Josie. She loves to be scratched on her neck. I think that's what she's trying to tell you," Gail said. "She's a lovebug. No need to be afraid."

Jerry ran his hand up and down Josie's neck, intrigued by the animal's warm solid body. Josie turned around to check him out. "You're a beautiful girl, aren't you? So pretty," he said, gazing into her eyes.

Jerry knew from his work at the Committee that cows had a range of emotions and behaviors, but when he'd seen them at other sanctuaries, they weren't very active. Josie, on the other hand, might jump in your lap, if you let her. Ironically, though he'd been vegan for twelve years, Jerry didn't hang out with animals very much, namely because of his allergies. He never had much of a chance to spend time with any to really appreciate their capacity for friendship. He was bonding with Josie in a way he never bonded with an animal before. It felt like a vegan baptism.

Then the girl cow dropped a formidable piece of dung, followed by a loud release of wind.

"That's your welcome present Uncle Jerry! A fresh Montana pie — with sound effects," Gail said as she walked over to him and put her hand on his shoulder. "Do you always have this effect on women?"

"Usually it takes a few dates before they really shit on me," Jerry exclaimed as he patted Josie on the stomach. "And that was enough methane to melt a polar ice cap."

Gail put her hands on her hips as she looked scornfully at him.

"Sorry, Josie, I didn't mean to embarrass you. That's just part of my global-warming schtik."

Gail imagined what it might be like to wake up in the morning next to this cute and funny vegan guy who was warming up so nicely to her and her animals. She was reminded of the crush she'd had on him in sixth grade. But he was oblivious to it back then, or so it seemed. And now, just when she was getting over her divorce and the loneliness of moving to a ranch two thousand miles away from home, Jerome Zuckerman walks back into her life. How incredible. After her ex, could she handle another Jewish guy?

First things first, she reminded herself. They would have dinner and plenty of time to talk. How much should she divulge about her prick of an ex-husband, the cardiac surgeon who had a years-long affair with the young tech in his practice? Would it make her look stupid? Or faithful? First things first. She just needed to chill out.

• • • •

As much as Gail thought about being careful not to send out romantic signals, she ended up putting together quite the cozy evening for her guest. Just walking into the timber house with its dormered ceiling and brick fireplace, Jerry felt like he was a special guest at an exclusive resort. The dining-room, with a sliding glass door leading out to a deck, overlooked the corral and the pasture, and there was still enough light outside to see the cows grazing and the mountainous skyline. Gail had put out the place settings earlier in the day and lit a single votive candle on the dining room table. A stereo in the living room, tuned to a public station, played an eclectic mix of jazz ballads and standards.

While Gail was in the bathroom washing up, Jerry looked at photos on the fireplace mantle. Most were of Eve and the cats, which still hadn't made an appearance. Unsurprisingly, none of the shots were of the ex-husband. Jerry wondered what the guy looked like. What was Gail's taste in men? Did she go for well-built lookers or scrawny cerebral types? Maybe her ex looked like Jerry — just a run of the mill Jewish guy.

After moving into the dining-room to check out the scenic view, the theme from the *MASH* television show, "Suicide is Painless," came on the radio. It was a cover by Bill Evans that Jerry had heard late one night on a radio station in Chicago a few years ago. Evans' interpretation was less melancholic and more breezy and adventurous than the original. The melody had been iconic during the 1970s, and hearing it again strongly stirred Jerry's emotions. For the second time that afternoon, he began to cry. It brought him right back to his childhood in Cleveland Heights — those same perfect days when he hung out with Gail at Irv's to enjoy a plate of French fries. He remembered having done an essay on the song for his tenth-grade music appreciation class, but he couldn't recall exactly what he had written — perhaps something anti-war, one of his favorite themes as a rebellious teenager.

While Gail warmed up the lasagna and cut up lettuce and tomatoes for a salad, she told Jerry about her career — going to John Carroll University, becoming a fifth-grade teacher, and then assistant principal at an elementary school in Euclid. "I was a year or two away from becoming principal when I found out Dick was having a long-term affair. The shock of it all really threw me."

"Really, his name was Dick?"

"Yep. Dr. Dick Silverman. All his pals just called him Dr. Dick." Gail said as she tossed the tomato slices and the lettuce into a clear glass bowl. "Completely self absorbed, but a great surgeon. People came from around the world to have him do their bypasses and valve replacements."

Gail opened the door of the refrigerator and pulled out a carafe. "I only have Italian dressing. I hope that's ok."

"Of course."

"You know, I wasn't completely surprised that he strayed. After twenty years of marriage, these things do happen, especially with doctors. But he admitted to having been with this girl on-and-off for three years. I just couldn't trust him after that. One of my friends saw them kissing in the hospital parking lot. That's how I found out."

"Wow," Jerry said. "He wasn't very discrete, was he?"

"I guess not. Anyway, let's forget about that mess and have dinner," Gail said just before grabbing a potholder and opening up the oven door to get the lasagna. "Now you just sit down so I can serve you."

Jerry obeyed, but waited for Gail to join him before putting the white cloth napkin on his lap. He couldn't remember the last time a woman, or anyone for that matter, cooked him a homemade meal. Had anyone ever even made him a vegan dinner before? "All that cow rustling got me hungry," Jerry said as Gail placed a large piece of lasagna on his plate. "I can't believe you made this wonderful dinner."

As calm and collected as she appeared to be, Gail began to feel a strong wave of emotion for Jerry coming over her. She had surrounded herself with the sanctuary and all its responsibilities to fill the void she felt after the divorce, but Jerry's presence for only a few hours made her realize that she wanted more. She wanted the intimacy and the sex and the exhilaration that comes with new love. Was she ready for it? What if it quickly fizzled or never materialized in the first place? There was no way to really know how to proceed. But with all the time they were about to spend together, physical intimacy seemed like a distinct possibility — that is, if Jerry was on board. But she needed to be careful not to rush things.

"Joey wasn't kidding about the lasagna," Jerry said after finishing his first bite. "Granted I eat take out a lot, but this is incredible, Gail. It's the tomato sauce, isn't it? The mushrooms, the spices. It tastes so fresh."

"Yep, you're right. I know this sounds kinda cliché, but it's adapted from an old Antonizzi recipe — from my great grandmother back in Italy. I've tried putting seitan and TVP in it as substitutes for the meat, but I think it's better without the protein. Except for a spice or two, all the ingredients are organic and local."

Gail poured Jerry a glass of red wine, which she noted was also organic and from a winery just outside of Missoula. "Not everyone out here gets what I'm doing — I mean this is carnivore country. But if I show the locals respect and patronize their businesses, I'm treated pretty well."

"Everything is so delicious," Jerry said as he chewed. "Sorry, I'm talking with my mouth full. Tomorrow night, you'll need to sequester me in the barn with Bonnie and Clyde."

Jerry began recounting his "almost married" story, the debacle with Missy, making a note to himself to leave out the part of having had a two-week affair with Claire, Missy's mom, after the engagement was broken off. He had sworn himself to absolute secrecy about his scandalous fling with her.

As he described his shock at seeing Missy eating chicken nuggets, "the beginning of the end" as he put it, Gail stopped him and pointed to the full moon cresting the mountains. "Sorry to interrupt, but I didn't want you to miss this. The previous owners told me that watching the full moon rise was a regular event for them. You picked the perfect day to come here, Jerr. It's great to share it with you." Jerry concurred, and though she tried not to get too caught up in the moment, her eyes began to water.

"I guess it was your turn to get a little weepy," Jerry said, handing her a clean napkin. "We vegans are such softies, aren't we?"

Gail nodded in agreement.

After clearing the table, they moved into the living room and sat side-by-side on the couch, talking a little, and listening to an ambient electronica program on the radio. The show's host — a subdued guy who sounded like Captain Cosmos, a space-music disc jockey who Jerry listened to every Sunday night in college — came on the air briefly to review the set list, which included works by musicians from Germany, Denmark, Iceland, and Japan. Gail eventually rested her head on Jerry's shoulder. A few minutes later, she turned her body into his, placing her hand on his chest. Before drifting off to sleep, she said, "I just wanted you to know I stopped shaving my legs. It's been very liberating. I know that's TMI, but I've been wanting to tell someone for forever."

"I'll make sure I update my records," Jerry said before touching her lightly on the forehead with his lips.

He was being drawn to Gail by a romantic force that was steadily getting stronger. Resisting it would soon be futile. He'd never imagined ending up in Montana with a courageous vegan woman who was starting a new life. But after being with her and the animals for a few hours, it began to feel right. Maybe it could work. If he stuck around for the long haul, he could fundraise. He could lead educational programs. He could shovel shit, which at the moment seemed strangely cathartic. And even though he'd be in the middle of nowhere, Starbucks was still just an hour away.

Jerry noticed one of the cats, a big grey tabby, standing in the hallway between the kitchen and the front door. Where did this hazard to his respiratory tranquility come from? It looked back at him with its tail slowly moving back and forth like a radar sweep. Maybe it was in search of a late-night snack. Maybe it wondered what this new human was doing in its house. Or maybe when it came down to it, the cat just didn't care.

About the Author

Ben Shaberman's essays, articles, and commentaries have been carried by several prominent media outlets including: *The Washington Post, Chicago Tribune, Baltimore Sun, VegNews, Vegetarian Times*, and NPR. He's also published fiction and creative non-fiction in a number of literary journals including: *Split Infinitive, Opium Magazine, Empty Mirror, The Good Men Project, Clean Sheets Erotica Magazine*, and *Crunchable.*

The Vegan Monologues, his collected essays, was published by Apprentice House in 2009.

Shaberman holds a master of arts in writing from Johns Hopkins University.

His awards include the Penny Ante Humor Scholarship from the Stonecoast Writers' Conference in 2003, and Second Place at the Des Moines National Poetry Festival in May 2002.

Acknowledgements

I'd like to thank the following people for their invaluable efforts and support:

Kevin Atticks

Keryl Cryer

Kaitlyn Gallagher

Sara Hammel

Kelley Murphy

Apprentice House is the country's only campus-based, student-staffed book publishing company. Directed by professors and industry professionals, it is a nonprofit activity of the Communication Department at Loyola University Maryland.

Using state-of-the-art technology and an experiential learning model of education, Apprentice House publishes books in untraditional ways. This dual responsibility as publishers and educators creates an unprecedented collaborative environment among faculty and students, while teaching tomorrow's editors, designers, and marketers.

Outside of class, progress on book projects is carried forth by the AH Book Publishing Club, a co-curricular campus organization supported by Loyola University Maryland's Office of Student Activities.

Eclectic and provocative, Apprentice House titles intend to entertain as well as spark dialogue on a variety of topics. Financial contributions to sustain the press' work are welcomed. Contributions are tax deductible to the fullest extent allowed by the IRS.

To learn more about Apprentice House books or to obtain submission guidelines, please visit www.apprenticehouse.com.

Apprentice House
Communication Department
Loyola University Maryland
4501 N. Charles Street
Baltimore, MD 21210
Ph: 410-617-5265 • Fax: 410-617-2198
info@apprenticehouse.com • www.apprenticehouse.com

www.ingramcontent.com/pod-product-compliance
Lightning Source LLC
LaVergne TN
LVHW051416080426
835508LV00022B/3115
* 9 7 8 1 6 2 7 2 0 0 7 9 0 *